9⁵⁄

MUSICALS

MUSICALS

The Guide to Amateur Production

Peter A. Spencer

Line illustrations by George Prescott

JOHN MURRAY

© Peter A. Spencer 1983

First published 1983
by John Murray (Publishers) Ltd
50 Albemarle Street, London W1X 4BD

Typeset by Inforum Ltd, Portsmouth
Printed in Great Britain by
Butler & Tanner Ltd, Frome and London

British Library Cataloguing in Publication Data
Spencer, Peter A.
Musicals : the guide to amateur production.
1. Musical revue, comedy, etc.—Amateur's manuals
I. Title
782.81   ML1950
ISBN 0-7195-4032-1

Contents

ACKNOWLEDGEMENTS

The author wishes to thank the following people for their help and advice in the preparation of this book: John Chandler, Bernard Dunn, Alan Leggett, Sydney Lockerman, Duncan McAra, Thelma Parish, George Prescott, Valerie Ripley, George Scott, Gill Tracy and Bill Whitebread; and The Wood Green Operatic Society for permission to reproduce the Rules of the Society. The extract from *Pink Champagne* by Eric Maschwitz and Bernard Grun is reprinted by kind permission of the publishers, Samuel French Ltd.

Illustrations

[1]

Overture and beginners, please!

Musicals – and I use the term to embrace musical comedies, operettas and light operas – are a universally enjoyed form of entertainment. The British, in particular, have taken them to their hearts, especially the tried and tested favourites, such as *My Fair Lady, Camelot, The King and I* and *The Sound of Music* and the perennial reissues of the film versions. BBC Radio has had several long-running series devoted to the musical theatre, for example *Nights of Gladness* and *Leading Ladies*.

A brief history of musicals

Whilst music has always played an important role in dramatic present-ations, the musical, as we know it today, really started as French *opérette* in the first half of the nineteenth century. Mark Lubbock attributes the invention of opérette to an eccentric musician named Florimond Ronger; he, however, preferred to call himself Hervé, and, on being appointed organist to a Parisian lunatic asylum, Hervé began to write little musical plays 'which the lunatics acted, the idea being to keep their minds off their morbid obsessions'! So effective did these prove that Hervé was offered the post of conductor at the Théâtre du Palais-Royal where he soon established himself as a successful composer of many shows in the new genre. But they did not stand the test of time and it took the genius of Jacques Offenbach to consolidate and develop Hervé's invention, and for over twenty-five years Offenbach was the unchallenged king of opérette. Many of his works, notably *Orpheus in the Underworld, La Belle Hélène* and *La Vie Parisienne*, are still popular today and regularly performed by both professional and amateur companies. Offenbach achieved international fame in his lifetime and, as his popularity grew, so did his demands for ever-increasing fees to the dismay of the Viennese theatre managers. Not until 1870 were they able to find an alternative 'home-grown' composer when, under intensive pressure from Maximilian Steiner and his own wife, Johann Strauss composed *Indigo or the Forty Thieves*.

Thus the Viennese Operetta was born and Strauss consolidated his initial success with fifteen more compositions, including the world-famous *The Gipsy Baron* and *Die Fledermaus*. Other composers followed his lead, notably Karl Millocker whose works include *The DuBarry*; Karl Zeller, who wrote *The Bird Seller*; and Richard Neuberger whose Chambre Séparée (from *The Opera Ball*) is in constant demand on request programmes. Composers in the modern Viennese school include Franz Lehar (*Frederica, The Land of Smiles* and *The Merry Widow*), Oscar Straus (*A Waltz Dream* and *The Chocolate Soldier*), Emmerich Kalman (*The Gipsy Princess*), Charles Cuvillier (*The Lilac Domino*), Robert Stolz (*Wild Violets*) and Heinrich Berté, who adapted Schubert's music for *Lilac Time*.

Meanwhile another school of operetta was developing in Berlin and the most famous to come from there were *White Horse Inn* (Ralph Benatzky) and *Viktoria and her Hussar* (Paul Abraham).

In England the ballad opera had existed since *The Beggar's Opera* (1728), and the romantic operas of the first half of the nineteenth century – *The Bohemian Girl* (1843) and *Maritana* (1845) – are still performed today. But English light opera really arrived with the collaboration of Gilbert and Sullivan in the Savoy Operas in 1877 and, for over twenty years, this partnership dominated the English musical stage. When Sullivan died in 1900, Edward German was called in to complete *The Emerald Isle* and he then went on to compose scores for *Merrie England, Tom Jones* and *A Princess of Kensington*. Others began to try their hand at comic opera, including Alfred Cellier (*Dorothy*), H. Fraser-Simpson (*The Maid of the Mountains*) and Montague Phillips (*The Rebel Maid*). Meanwhile, at the Gaiety Theatre, George Edwardes was establishing the musical comedy. The first show in this new form *In Town* (1892), which transferred from the Prince of Wales Theatre, was followed by *The Shop Girl* in 1894. Then came a succession of 'girl' shows which included *The Circus Girl, The Runaway Girl, The Quaker Girl* and *A Country Girl*.

For the first half of the twentieth century, Britain was the home of musicals. Notable highlights were the long-running production of *Chu Chin Chow* at His Majesty's; Ivor Novello's spectacular productions at Drury Lane; *Salad Days*; *The Boy Friend*; and many more right up to today's Tim Rice and Andrew Lloyd Webber collaborations such as *Jesus Christ Superstar* and *Evita*.

The greatest influence on the modern musical has undoubtedly come from the United States. Initially imported shows from Europe held sway and an American musical comedy did not emerge until the arrival of the twentieth century. The credit for this must go to George M. Cohan, a librettist, lyricist and composer. His basic formula, which was adhered to for many years, was an opening chorus of girls, big production numbers to close each act, boy always gets girl, villain always gets his just desserts and the stars are allowed to do their own thing. The story, as such, was of minor importance. Nevertheless, despite these restrictions, many of the early musicals did manage to achieve some distinction. In 1927, with *Show Boat*, there arrived a musical play, as opposed to a musical comedy, where everything was subservient to the plot. At last, according to David Ewen in *The Complete Book of Light Opera*, there was a show which had 'a consistent and credible story line, authentic atmosphere and three-dimensional characters'.

The next milestone was Rodgers and Hammerstein's *Oklahoma!* (1943) with which the American musical play became an American art form. From that date the ascendancy of the American musical has continued unchecked with works coming from the pen of Cole Porter, Leonard Bernstein, Irving Berlin, Lerner and Loewe and Stephen Sondheim to cite but a few. One American show has officially been designated a 'classic' when, in 1982, *Guys and Dolls* was given a National Theatre production. In the same year, the USA sent to London their Broadway version of *The Pirates of Penzance*!

Writers of musicals draw their inspiration from a variety of sources as the following examples illustrate. Biographies have yielded up *The Mitford Girls, Barnum* and *Marilyn*; literature has been the source of *The Man of la Mancha, Pickwick* and *Jorrocks* and many plays have been adapted — *The Barretts of Wimpole Street, Blithe Spirit*, and *Gaslight* being three that come to mind. At least five strip cartoons have formed the basis of musicals — *Annie, Andy Capp, Li'l Abner, You're a Good Man Charlie Brown* and *Snoopy*; Fellini's film $8\frac{1}{2}$ has been transformed into *Nine* while T.S. Eliot's book of poems, *Old Possum's Book of Practical Cats*, is the inspiration for Andrew Lloyd Webber's musical, *Cats*.

Professional companies are showing a renewed interest in the older musicals. Several of the Gilbert and Sullivan canon have been given a new lease of life with up-to-date modern staging; the New Sadler's Wells Opera is presenting seasons of operetta and has already mounted new productions of *The Count of Luxembourg, Countess Maritza* and *The Mikado* whilst *Mr Cinders* was revived after over fifty years at the end of 1982.

The amateur movement

To trace the beginnings of the British amateur stage movement one must go back to the Mystery Plays of the twelfth century. Although priests originally played the parts they were soon supplanted by ordinary working folk from the Guilds who, whilst sometimes receiving small payments for their services, were not regular professional players.

Masques were the recreation of the Court and the big country houses and, in 1558, Elizabeth I attended a performance of *Gorbuduc*, written and performed by the gentlemen of the Inner Temple.

During Victoria's reign home amateur theatricals were the rage of the middle and upper classes and, in 1842, The Old Stagers, arguably the oldest amateur dramatic society, was founded. Others followed and the popularity of the Savoy Operas encouraged many to widen their scope to include musical productions.

On 15 February 1899, at the Grosvenor Hotel in Manchester, representatives of eleven societies met to form the National Amateur Operatic and Dramatic Association (NODA). Nine months later the first Annual General Meeting took place, at which forty-one societies were represented. The Association was founded 'to bring together members of operatic and dramatic societies to promote their common interest in amateur theatre'. Numbers climbed steadily for twenty years and then, between 1920–30, membership boomed and the total of affiliates rose to 1,000. Since the Second World War NODA has flourished and current membership exceeds 1,500 societies. The majority of these are within the United Kingdom but there are members in Australia, Bahamas, Belgium, Canada, West Germany, Gibraltar, Jamaica, New Zealand, Portugal, South Africa, Switzerland, USA, Zambia and Zimbabwe. Even so, these groups are nearly all founded by ex-patriates who were carrying on the British tradition, which is probably unique in its size, scope and organisation. Only in the United States can one find a comparable movement and there it is centred upon the colleges and universities and in many cases is semi-professional.

However this is not the full total. There are others involved in musical productions – members of the armed forces, youth clubs, schools and other organisations – who, for one reason or another, are not affiliated to NODA. I would make a conservative estimate that between 2,000 – 2,500 groups in the UK are involved in amateur musical productions.

In recent years there has been a growing interest in exchange visits with overseas companies. The Grosvenor Light Opera Company, which specialises in traditional productions of the Gilbert and Sullivan operas, has for many years taken productions to the Continent. In 1980 the Central Council for Amateur Theatre estimated that 14,000,000 tickets were sold for amateur productions in the United Kingdom and it is believed that this figure continues to increase.

Amateur musical productions cost a great deal of money. Commenting on the amateur musical movement in *The Times* in 1980, Cyril Bainbridge noted that 'sums as high as £15,000 can be involved'. And costs are rising. It is natural, therefore, that box-office appeal plays a great part in the selection of shows and most amateur companies tend to be conservative in their choice. In a list of over 470 productions scheduled for the first five months of 1982, I counted 20 *Carousel*, 18 *Fiddler on the Roof*, 17 *The Merry Widow* and 15 *Annie Get Your Gun*. But fashions change rapidly, since in the summer issue of *NODA News*, just six months previously, the top five favourite shows were listed as *The Merry Widow*, *The Mikado*, *The Gondoliers*, *Iolanthe* and *The Desert Song*.

Nevertheless some more adventurous companies will attempt new shows, encouraged by the authors who wish to try out their work, with a view to having it taken up by a professional producer. Recently there have been amateur premières of *Pudding Lane* (based on the Great Fire of London) and *The Rothschilds*. Some groups make a speciality of presenting Broadway shows which have never crossed to these shores as professional productions — *Tenderloin* is an example. Others concentrate on rarely performed works such as *The Bird Seller*, *Lisa* or *The Beggar Student*.

School productions

Schools have long appreciated the value of the musical production as an additional educational tool. In the last decade many have broken away from the diet of Gilbert and Sullivan operas and tackled the more demanding technicalities of shows such as *Oliver!*, *Anne of Green Gables* and *Oh What a Lovely War!* A deputy headmistress, who is also head of the drama department of a large comprehensive school in south-west England, told me: 'A musical is an ideal project since it incorporates so many departments apart from the immediately obvious art, music and drama classes.' One should choose shows where large numbers are involved and the children will vie with one another to be included in the cast or the technical crew. It has been observed that these productions have a beneficial, psychological effect upon the students. Musicals used as a school project have the added advantage that the end product – the performance – is appreciated by pupils, parents and staff alike.

The future of the amateur movement

Writers, composers and professional actors have come to acknowledge the value of the amateur movement in fostering an interest in and dedication to the theatre. In a recent inquiry into the future of light opera by the Arts Council of Great Britain it was noted that '. . . the better amateur companies are at least the equal of professional touring companies' and, in many places, amateurs provide the only live theatre available.

Stage productions, both amateur and professional, are becoming increasingly expensive to mount and all involve a high degree of risk. On 14 February 1983 there were sixteen West End theatres 'dark' – the sad trade euphemism for closed – and in the past decade many amateur groups, faced with continual losses, have been forced to disband. On the brighter side we have noted that full houses can still be achieved by societies maintaining a high standard of production backed by good publicity.

Apart from participating in shows amateurs should support professional and amateur productions and encourage their friends to do likewise. Regular theatre-going is a habit. It should be implanted at an early age and the influence of both parents and schools cannot be over-emphasised in this respect. A continual search for excellence coupled with active audience support will ensure the healthy future of both the amateur and professional theatre.

This book is offered in the hope that it will give members of existing companies a greater understanding of the techniques of the productions which they enjoy, and that it will act as a useful tool for the newcomer to the fascinating world of the musical theatre. It is distilled from over thirty years' practical experience of acting and directing amateurs and represents a very personal view. For this reason it should be read in conjunction with other titles listed in the bibliography and in the light of one's own experience.

[2]

The company and the production staff

Amateur operatic companies

The hard core of amateur operatic societies are affiliated to the National Operatic and Dramatic Association. It is the only organisation of its kind in the world and its energies are devoted to the amateur musical and dramatic theatre in both hemispheres. Membership is available to both companies and individuals and full details may be obtained by writing to the General Administrator at NODA's head office at 1 Crestfield Street, London WC1H 8HU.

The many benefits that membership of NODA confers, and which are of particular interest to the production team, include the free use of their extensive library of over 30,000 volumes. These cover every aspect of production and include libretti and vocal and orchestral scores, as well as a set of comprehensive synopses of over 100 operas and musical shows. New scores and libretti are available to members at generous discounts. In addition, NODA gives free legal advice, finds substitute players in an emergency and arranges insurance schemes for a show at advantageous premiums.

They also act as agents for directors and musical directors. A free publication, *NODA News*, is available to all members. As well as containing full details of current and forthcoming amateur productions, this newspaper provides valuable information on new releases, new and unusual professional productions, technical news, legal and governmental proposals that could be of importance, and numerous articles on all aspects of the amateur theatre. Both members of the production staff and individual company members would well be advised to join this Association.

Management of an amateur company

In most cases the Constitution and Rules of an amateur musical company will be based on the model suggested by NODA. The Wood Green Operatic Society in north London is one such company and I am indebted to their General Management Committee for allowing me to quote at length from their rules, which appear in the appendix on pp. 151–5. The day-to-day running of the society is in the hands of the GMC which comprises officers and other elected members of the company.

Of these, those with whom the production team will have most dealings are the secretary, the business manager, the treasurer and the publicity manager. The main link with the management committee is the secretary who will confirm the appointment of the production team, see that the rehearsal rooms are booked, that rehearsal accompanists are engaged and ensure that members of the company are made aware of the rehearsal calls. He, or more often she, will organise auditions, obtain libretti and scores, deal with any legal aspect of the production and attend to the formalities regarding the use of children in a show, as well as with insurance and copyright matters.

Usually the business manager will confine his duties to all aspects relating to the production in hand. It is he who will normally issue the contracts for the hire of scenery, costumes and lighting equipment and any properties or furniture required.

The director should liaise with the publicity manager on matters of advertising so that the company's publicity reflects the style of production which he has in mind. Such questions as the billing credits or the synopsis of scenes should be discussed, as a director's ideas can vary from those in the published acting editions. (The publicity manager is also responsible for front of house decoration and photographs.)

The production team will be considered in detail in ensuing chapters, but a word on its composition is appropriate here. Apart from the director, all or some of the following will be included in the team: musical director, chorus master, choreographer or dancing mistress, stage manager, assistant stage manager(s), company electrician, stage carpenter, designer, art director, lighting designer, property master, wardrobe mistress, accompanists, prompter, call boy(s) or girl(s), makeup artist and sound and effects engineers.

With the possible exception of the director, musical director and choreographer, most of the members of this team will be drawn from the society. Some of the duties listed may be combined; for example, the musical director may act as chorus master while the stage manager may attend to the devising and recording of the sound effects.

In long-established companies, particularly those specialising in the performance of musical comedies, the members will fall broadly into four groups: principals, chorus, dancers and extras. Usually the principals will have graduated from the chorus, although, in certain cases, outsiders may be recruited to play leading roles. Membership is normally through an acting or vocal audition and, in the case of singers, one will be allocated a place according to one's voice range. Dancers are selected for their dancing ability and may be required to audition for every show to demonstrate their prowess in the style of dancing required in a particular production. They may also be choristers and revert to the chorus when not required in the dancing team.

Extras, as their name implies, are recruited from any available source to 'dress' the stage as footmen, flunkeys or waiters, or they may be asked to play small 'walk-on' parts when it is undesirable to deplete the vocal strength by allocating the role to a chorister.

In addition there will be a number of active members who confine their interest to the technical and management aspects of the production. These lines of demarcation are less strongly drawn in the companies who play modern American-type musicals. In such societies one would expect most of the singers to be able to dance and act, and most of the dancers to be able to hold a vocal line and be able to play a small role, whilst a principal player in one show may well revert to the ensemble for the following production.

Financial considerations

INCOME

(1) Membership fees: These range from a small weekly subscription to £35.00 or more per year. (In the Greater London Council area these fees are entirely swallowed up by the Evening Institute fee.)

In many areas of the UK, established musical societies can become affiliated to an Evening Institute and run their company as an Evening Class. A fee is paid for every active (as opposed to honorary) member and, in return, the local authority provide the rehearsal premises, usually in a school and, subject to the number of individuals under instruction, will pay the fees of the director, musical director, choreographer and pianist, all of whom they will consider as part-time teachers. Unfortunately these concessions function only during the 'term time' and do not include 'school holidays'. Since production schedules extend over many months the company has to pay for rehearsals which take place outside 'term time'. Many societies have considered the alternative and decided that only by joining an Evening Class can they remain viable. It should be noted that although an Evening Class, the society can still audition prospective members and reject any that do not come up to their standards.

(2) Sale of tickets: By far the largest source of income.

(3) Sale of programmes.

(4) Revenue from advertisements in programmes.

(5) Local subsidies.

(6) Local Arts Committee grants.

(7) Sale of refreshments at rehearsals and performances.

(8) Other activities during the society's year, e.g. social events.

(9) Donations.

EXPENDITURE

(1) Performing fees: Unless the show is out of copyright, or it has been specially commissioned for the company without fee, royalties are always payable. These may be a fixed sum per performance, but more often are calculated as a percentage of the box office returns – $12\frac{1}{2}\%$ being the average charged.

(2) Production staff (director, musical director and choreographer): In the majority of cases these people will be paid a fee. If services are given free of charge, out-of-pocket and travelling expenses may be paid.

(3) Rehearsal pianist(s): It is not unusual to have two or three accompanists to cover chorus, principals and dancing rehearsals. If paid, the same remarks apply as in the previous section.

(4) Vocal scores, libretti and band parts: Scores and libretti are getting increasingly expensive; £7.00 for a score and £1.50 for a libretto is not uncommon today. NODA is currently offering a 15% discount on these items to its members and it is also possible to hire scores from NODA. An alternative is to buy second-hand (*NODA News* features this service in the classified columns) and subsequently re-sell, or for individuals to obtain copies from their local library, although one can hardly supply a complete company in this way. On no account should photocopies be made since this is illegal and could result in heavy

damages. Band parts, if required, will have to be hired (even for the Gilbert and Sullivan operas) and a returnable deposit paid.

(5) Rehearsal accommodation: Unless the company is fortunate enough to have its own club room or theatre, sooner or later rehearsal rooms will need to be hired. Initial music rehearsals and principal read-throughs can be managed in private houses, but staging and dancing rehearsals will require floor space equivalent to the area of the stage where the performance will take place. Rehearsal rooms should be equipped with a good piano.

(6) The performance: Whether the performance is held in a theatre or local hall, there will be a rental and this may or may not include extras such as resident stage crew, electricity, overtime, etc.

(7) Scenery: Hire charges, transport and VAT apply. If making one's own, we assume the possession of flats, cloths, rostra, etc, and the facilities to make and paint the sets. Nevertheless there will still be some expense for paint, size, screws and nails and the like.

(8) Costumes and wigs: As in the previous paragraph, these may be hired or the company may possess a large and comprehensive wardrobe with facilities to alter and fit the costumes and dress the wigs. Even so, it will be a lucky company who has the ability to dress every show completely.

(9) Makeup: Many companies engage makeup artists for a fee. Even when the work is done by talented specialists within the society, makeup will need replenishing and is very expensive.

(10) Lighting: Even in a fully equipped theatre, a musical production invariably requires additional lighting equipment to be hired.

(11) Furniture and properties: Charges will depend on the style and period of the show. The cost for *Die Fledermaus* or *The DuBarry*, with their rich period interiors, will be much higher than for *Oklahoma!* or *Finian's Rainbow*.

(12) Sound effect and amplification: Professional theatres may carry this equipment but it could be a fairly big expense if required in a local hall.

(13) Orchestra: Theatres will usually insist on players being members of the Musicians' Union, and Union rates will have to be paid. If an amateur orchestra is used, out-of-pocket and travelling expenses may have to be met. If pianos are used, they will need to be tuned at least once. Orchestra stands, fitted with lights, may also have to be hired.

(14) Printing and publicity: The cost of printing tickets, programmes, handbills, order forms, posters, the cost of newspaper

advertisements and any fees for poster sites. When playing at a professional theatre this last cost is sometimes included in the contract.

(15) Insurance: A small premium will cover against injury to any member of the company and loss or damage to any of the hired goods – costumes, furniture, properties, etc.

(16) Other incidentals: A sum – around 10% of the total expenditure – is usually set aside to cover the cost of decorating the front of house, photographs, flowers, tips and 'thank you' gifts, free tickets to the press and the entertainment of VIPs.

All together a formidable list which can total anything from £1,000 to well over £20,000 for a week's run of a show. The production crew who can cut some of these costs, while at the same time not jeopardising the artistic integrity of the show, will endear themselves to the GMC and to the business manager and treasurer in particular.

Choosing a musical show

'This is a problem which invariably results in a traumatic session by every society, every season.' (*NODA News*, Vol 39 No 2, 1981.)

The question that always arises is: 'Is it box-office?' For, with the majority of companies, it is essential that each show pays its way, or, at the very least, breaks even.

Large, old-established companies in areas where a strong community spirit exists should enjoy a greater freedom of choice. Yet even they may find their audience conservative in the shows which they will patronise.

Ideally, a society should build up a reputation for excellence so that the audience will attend, no matter what show is presented.

The fact remains however, that, although there are well over 400 musical shows released for amateur production, selection is made from a very small percentage of the available titles.

Who chooses the show? In some cases it is done autocratically by a dominant personality (the chairman, resident musical director or the director). More often it is done democratically by an elected committee with, in some cases, final selection by the members of the society. Whatever system is adopted, here are a few guidelines to show selection, suggested by NODA:

(1) Get a firm booking at a theatre in the form of a contract, having paid the required deposit and obtained, if necessary, a licence from the local authority. This establishes some basic criteria, such as staging limitations and box-office potential.

(2) Select the type of show appropriate to the company's talent, e.g. Gilbert and Sullivan, operetta, old or modern musicals. List possible titles in the selected category – members and even audience could be consulted.

(3) Consider the production team – must the show suit them or will they be chosen to suit the show?

(4) Consider the possibilities in the selected category and produce a short list of probables, taking into account casting, chorus and dancing potential, staging limitations, orchestral requirements, costumes, scenery and, inevitably, financial budget.

(5) Using this short list, check with the publishers, performing rights' holders or their agents that the shows are available (another society may already have a contract in your locality or the show may be temporarily withdrawn), and ensure that the scores, libretti and band-parts are readily available.

(6) Check with other societies in the locality where you perform – they may also have the show on their short list! (In fairness to rights' holders, it must be a case of first come, first served.)

(7) Check that the scenery and costumes for each show are available *and ask the traders to pencil in your dates*.

(8) Now make your final choice and get a firm contract to perform; obtain the scores and libretti, book the scenery, costumes, orchestra, etc, and cancel previously pencilled bookings.

(9) Reconsider your budget – which probably means putting up your seat prices.

The production team

A good musical director should have a thorough knowledge of musical notation and the ability to instruct and conduct an orchestra. He should also possess a good 'stick' technique and have a knowledge of voice production and singing techniques. (Incidentally, the last two are valuable attributes for a director, as we shall see.)

It is not unusual to find that the musical director of a company is more or less a permanent fixture, whereas directors and choreographers tend to be engaged show by show. The post is usually held by a man, although talented women are beginning to take up the baton. Some societies have a chorus master to teach the notes to the ensemble, leaving the musical director free to concentrate on the principals in the initial stages before taking over command to polish and blend the whole show.

In either case it is essential to have the musical director in attendance at entrance auditions. Great care should be taken to place successful entrants in their correct voice range: first soprano, second soprano, first alto, second alto, first tenor, second tenor, baritone or bass. This is important since some of the older shows call for these subdivisions, and it must be assumed that once an entrant has been accepted he or she will stay with the company for many shows. Initially singers in the same voice group sit together at rehearsals, the better to instruct and control them.

The choreographer will be a trained dancer. Usually a woman she may have graduated from the ranks of the society, be a local dancing teacher or a graduate from one of the nationally established dance colleges. She can be employed regularly by the society or a new choreographer may be engaged show-by-show depending on the type of dancing required. Sometimes the director will arrange his own choreography.

At the head of this team is the director. I stress the term 'team'. It is essential that these three specialists work together with complete understanding, each respecting the expertise of the other and working in concert for the good of the show. Should there be dissension, it is the director who has the last word – but I have never found it necessary to invoke this privilege.

In his book *On the Art of the Theatre*, Edward Gordon Craig wrote: 'It is neither acting nor the play, it is not scene nor dance, but it consists of all the elements of which these things are composed: action, which is the very spirit of acting; words, which are the body of the play; line and colour, which are the very heart of the scene; rhythm, which is the very essence of the dance.'

The director's task is to control these various elements. He must guide the large body of individuals involved in a musical show, and weld them into a corporate body. He is, above all, responsible for the artistic and dramatic integration of the production.

The ideal director, states the *Oxford Companion to the Theatre*, 'must be an actor, an artist, an architect, an electrician, an expert in geography, history, costume, accessories and scenery, and have a thorough understanding of human nature – the last trait being the most essential'.

The director of opera, operette, musical comedy or musical play requires two additional prime qualifications: a love and knowledge of music and an appreciation of choreography.

Acquiring the basic knowledge

Before the demise of so many of our local theatres it was a comparatively simple matter to cultivate the acquaintance of a friendly stage manager who would let one watch him at work and thus get a basic grounding in the mechanics of the stage. Today, alas, such opportunities are rare. There are a number of specialist schools which, together, make up the Conference of Drama Schools. The courses they offer run over two or three years and include training in acting techniques, fencing, historical dance, television techniques, lighting and stage management and instruction for potential teachers of drama. These courses are aimed chiefly at the serious student who intends to make a career of the acting profession, although some schools do claim to provide a good foundation for the aspiring director.

An alternative is to undertake any role or job in as many varied amateur productions as possible, thus gaining an insight into the requirements of a director at other people's expense. Be prepared to undertake stage management, help with the scene painting, try your skill at making stage properties, in fact do anything that will help you to build up a store of knowledge and experience from which you will eventually need to draw. The annual Summer School run by NODA for its members includes sections for directors. Most local libraries contain books on aspects of the theatre which are worth reading. I have also found it advantageous to subscribe to a number of specialist publications in order to keep abreast of current trends in stage lighting and new musical shows (see Bibliography).

In addition see as many productions, both professional and amateur, as your funds will allow. Go, not only for the enjoyment of the show, but to study the techniques of the actors, the stage groupings, the settings and the lighting. Every show can teach one something, even if it is what should be avoided. A show directed by one of the recognised great directors is worthy of more than one visit.

In the majority of cases it is the company that chooses its director, musical director and choreographer. Selection can be in a variety of ways but is generally made by the General Management Committee. This body may offer these positions to members of the company who have demonstrated their ability, or they may make approaches to established exponents whose work they have witnessed, or request NODA to suggest suitable candidates. Appointments are made for a specific show or for a specified season.

Fees

One is sometimes required to attend an interview with the GMC to discuss one's experience, methods, rehearsal requirements and fee, if any. Fees can range from out-of-pocket expenses to several hundreds of pounds depending on experience, whether the director both directs and choreographs, and whether the company is affiliated to an Evening Class when the fees will be paid by the local authority.

When agreeing a fee, be certain to clarify whether the sum is an inclusive figure or whether travelling expenses and extra rehearsals will be charged.

The initial readings and the production conference

Once appointed, all the production team should study the script and become acquainted with the score. At this stage each is aiming at a general understanding of the piece. (If you have ever painted in oils, this is comparable to the initial blocking-in of the canvas. One is seeking an overall conception and there is no reference to detail.)

If a musical is the result of an adaptation of a book or play, reference to the original work may yield useful information, e.g. *Pygmalion* for *My Fair Lady*; *Oliver Twist* for *Oliver!*; *The Front Page* for *Windy City*.

One can also see a professional production of the piece or listen to a recording of the show (there is a large and growing collection of LPs covering musicals) always providing that one uses these as learning aids and does not regard them as definitive performances.

As one researches, an idea of the finished production begins to emerge but this picture must be tempered with other considerations: the size and strength of the company, the facilities available at the hall or theatre, the budget and the expectations of the local audience. A word of explanation on the latter point. Does the audience expect to see a reproduction of the original West End show or will it accept a new approach? Is it a sophisticated audience which will not object to seeing a production on a thrust stage with minimal symbolic settings and all the trappings of modern lighting technology in full view, or does it expect the traditional proscenium stage, the elaborate settings, with all technical equipment hidden from sight?

Having studied the show from their own viewpoint, the production team meet for the first production conference where they pool ideas and discuss at length how the show will be staged. Whatever his ideas, the director must consider the needs of both the choreographer and the musical director, paying particular attention to the positioning of the singers and the provision of sufficient space for the dancers. The stage manager, who should be present at this meeting, will be able to advise on the practicability of any staging ideas raised, and all should give full consideration to his remarks.

In addition to discussing the technical side, the team should voice their ideas regarding the aesthetic conception of the show. Every idea propounded should be argued out, and any suggestion that is not logically viable should be discounted; there should be no change for the sake of change. None of this reduces the director's influence on the finished work; but, unlike his counterpart in the legitimate theatre, he is one of a team. He should be the guiding force and he is the one who will ultimately have to make all the decisions.

Several production conferences are necessary before an interpretation emerges, embracing all the departments of acting, singing, dancing and staging. The team will now have a general conception of the finished product; the details will be hammered out in the long weeks of rehearsal ahead, and during this period there must be a constant interchange of ideas. But now each can start on his or her area of concern, working along converging lines which meet at the final rehearsals, and from now on we will follow each independently until their efforts recombine.

[3]

Starting at ground level

Having established the overall general conception of the show, the director will want to begin preparing his prompt book, but first he must settle two important points: the size and amenities of the hall or theatre where the production will be staged, and the scenic plots. The latter will, to a large measure, be dictated by the former.

The development of musical settings

The older musicals were written in two, three or four acts, each comprising one set. Box sets were used for interiors and backcloths, wings and borders for the exteriors. Scene changes were made in the intervals hidden from the public gaze by the House Curtain. The Savoy Operas, *Lilac Time, The Quaker Girl* and *The Vagabond King* fall into this category.

In the 1930s settings became more and more lavish. *White Horse Inn* used not only the huge stage of the London Coliseum but parts of the auditorium as well. Assorted live animals, stage bands, lake steamers and a torrential thunderstorm were involved in the spectacle, which made use of revolves and included an orchestra of over 100 musicians. The acts were broken down into a number of scenes, alternating between full stage and front cloth settings. The latter could be flown in and the action of the play continue whilst the main stage was reset. Changes – even the lowering of the cloth – were still normally hidden from the sight of the audience by the use of trailers or blackouts.

Ivor Novello was the leading British composer of this period and his lavish shows are still firm favourites with amateur companies and continue to attract good box-offices. *King's Rhapsody, The Dancing Years* and *Perchance to Dream* are three examples.

For centuries the traditional materials for scenery had been wood and canvas but, in the middle of the twentieth century, engineering techniques and materials, coupled with vastly improved electronics, began to be widely used. One of the innovators in this field was Sean Kelly who designed Lionel Bart's *Oliver!* where scene changes took place in full view of the audience, and *Blitz* where huge, automated slabs of scenery moved about the stage under the guidance of drivers concealed within them. Composers of musicals, realising that they were no longer tied to the old conventional two- or three-act shows, began to introduce ever more locales into their work, and designers were stretched to find means of achieving quick, silent scene changes.

Automated trucks, and bridges, multi-slide back projections, film, illuminated tilted floors, mirrored back walls and all the machinery of a vast factory have been utilised in such recent productions as *A Little Night Music, I and Albert, Evita, Jesus Christ Superstar, A Chorus Line* and *Sweeney Todd*.

In the recent production of *Cats* the whole theatre is used. Parts of the auditorium, including the seated audience, revolve around the main acting area; entrances are made from all parts of the house, including spectacular arrivals from the roof, from beneath the seats and through the backcloth itself. Every known technique appears to have been regimented into this piece of 'theatre'. *Cats* is an excellent example of what an imaginative talent can devise and is a lesson to all would-be directors, and like *Barnum*, another superbly staged musical, it demands far greater skills of its cast than the usual singing, acting and dancing abilities.

These types of setting require much expensive equipment and take a great deal of time and labour to install. Nevertheless, the director should be aware of the techniques used today since he may, albeit in a smaller, less grandiose manner, be able to introduce them into his own work one day.

The amateur's stage

The facilities offered by the hall or theatre where the production is to be performed will obviously have a bearing upon the type of setting that one can employ. Since the Second World War we have seen the closure and demolition of far too many theatres, music halls and cinemas which served as homes for local amateur companies. A few theatres have been restored – Edinburgh, Manchester and Nottingham come to mind, and a number of civic theatres have been built in recent years. It is essential that the director and the officers of societies keep themselves informed of any local plans to create a civic theatre and get themselves involved with

discussions at an early date to present their views and special requirements. Even when only modification to an existing theatre or hall is
envisaged, it is imperative that the technicians, who are going to work
in that venue, voice their opinions. Such timely action would have
prevented one local London authority from constructing a new scenic
dock with an opening 15 ft 6 in. (4.72 m) high for a stage where the
standard height of scenery used was 16 ft (4.87 m).

The majority of amateur musicals are still played in proscenium
settings and while we shall be considering performing in the round and
thrust stage techniques later in this chapter it may be of value to consider
the facilities offered in a traditional theatre.

THE STAGE will be of wood and will be flat save in very exceptional
circumstances when there may be a rake from back to front. Rakes create
problems for the designer since, unless one uses wedges, the scenery will
tilt towards the audience and all vertical lines will be out of true. In
addition, stage trucks and wheeled properties will have a tendency to
creep downstage – sometimes with disastrous results. However, I have
read that ballet dancers find the slope an aid to their elevation.

THE ACTING AREA, the part of the stage on which the actor appears,
should be in clear view from all parts of the auditorium and is
determined by the seating arrangements of the house and the sight-lines
from those seats.

THE WORKING AREA or WING SPACE, the area at the sides of the acting
area, should be large enough to accommodate the packs of flats required
in the show, the trucks, furniture, properties and other equipment, as
well as allowing space for the chorus to assemble.

THE PROSCENIUM OPENING is the picture frame through which the
audience see the play. It is often referred to as the 'fourth wall'. Often, a
false proscenium is built upstage of this to serve as a setting edge for
sets. Behind the adjustable border the all-important No. 1 spot bar is
usually hung.

THE PROMPT CORNER is, by tradition, downstage left, whether or not
the prompter actually sits there. It is usually the working corner where
the stage manager will have his desk and cue board, and from whence he
controls the entire running of the show. Should circumstances dictate

that the working corner and the prompter are located on stage right, it is referred to as a 'bastard prompt'.

ELECTRICIAN'S SWITCHBOARD in the past was usually on a steel gantry, some 8 ft above stage level, on the side of the stage, where the chief electrician and his assistants would juggle with a complicated array of switches, dimmers and interlocking gears. They could see little of the stage action and relied on verbal cues. Today most lighting control is done from a sound-proof booth in the auditorium, giving the lighting technician a clear view of the stage.

THE FLIES is the space high above the stage where scenery, cloths and drapes are hung when not in use; it gets its name because scenery 'flies up there'.

THE GRID is an open framework of wood or metal, hung high above the stage and covering the whole of the stage area, from which suspended scenery is hung. In the grid are mounted the pulley blocks over which the lines that carry the scenery will travel. Each batten or barrel is suspended on three lines, the long, centre and short, respectively – the short line being the one nearest to the fly rail.

THE FLY-FLOOR is a gallery running along the sides of the stage above the wing space, providing a working space from which to operate the lines of the grid and ensuring that the stage area is kept free of the clutter of ropes. It is protected by a heavily built fly rail which carries two rows of cleats, an upper and a lower. When the cloth has been hung squarely at its correct height it is made off, or 'deaded', to the lower cleat. When not required, the cloth is flown out of sight. The lines are not taken off the bottom cleat, but hauled from above it, and when the cloth is at a sufficient height, the lines are made off, in a bight, on the upper cleat.

There may be a fly-floor on either side of the stage but usually the prompt side is used for tying-off.

This practice applies to the so-called hand-worked or rope houses, where the scenery was raised manually. Nowadays wire ropes and counterweights using a system of brakes are employed, and under this system the fly gallery may be done away with.

SCENE DOCK is a bay opening off the stage proper where scenery is stored. It usually has large double doors opening onto the street.

PROPERTY ROOM. Here are stored all items which do not come under the heading of scenery, wardrobe or lighting — items such as carpets, pictures, flowers and, surprisingly, animals.

In addition one may find a *Furniture Store* and a *Quick-Change Room*. If the theatre has a revolve or trap doors, the mechanism for operating these will be housed below the stage where there may also be found the *Band Room*. Access to the orchestra pit is also normally via the under-stage area.

Some idea of the wealth of facilities that can be provided may be gauged from the following details of one of the USA's largest houses. The Metropolitan Opera House, New York, boasts a main stage 100 ft wide by 83 ft deep, in which there are seven lifts. There are three slip stages — one on the right of the stage measuring 60 ft by 48 ft; one on the left measuring 60 ft by 40 ft and another at the rear of the main stage area. All move automatically and are capable of carrying a complement of full sets plus cast.

103 sets of electrically controlled pre-set lines are available for hanging scenery in addition to the electrical lines. A cyclorama 109 ft by 270 ft can completely surround the main stage and there is an orchestra pit that can seat up to 110 musicians at any playing level!

A valuable guide to the technical facilities available in most theatres in the UK is the *British Theatre Directory*, published by Vance-Offord (Publications) Ltd of Eastbourne.

It is clear, from reference to *NODA News* Fixture List that, for every amateur company that enjoys the amenities of a real theatre, there are a score that have to perform in a school hall, community centre or town hall, the majority of which were designed for a variety of purposes other than stage productions. Consequently, the director must be prepared to contend with a stage of minimal dimensions, often complete lack of headroom or wing space together with rudimentary lighting equipment. There is seldom an orchestra pit and the seating arrangements in an unraked auditorium will give trouble with sight-lines.

He must therefore become a master of compromise and adaptation.

When working in a new venue, he should, at the earliest opportunity, visit it to acquaint himself with the layout and the existing facilities. It is an excellent idea to obtain a scaled plan and elevation of the stage and the auditorium with these technical details clearly indicated. Thus armed, he can begin to consider sets and draw up his ground plans.

The scenery

All scenery is a deception and theatre audiences accept the convention of suspended belief and willingly enter into the spirit of make-believe. Scenery can range from the starkly symbolic to the most naturalistic and, ideally, every production should be specially designed for the particular stage on which it is played. The design is a collaboration between the director and the scene designer, costume designer and lighting designer, who may sometimes be one and the same person. All should study the text to discover what the author has to say about the settings. The information will vary widely: the two acts of *The Mikado* are described as: 'Courtyard of Ko-Ko's Palace in Titipu' and 'Ko-Ko's Garden'. The libretto of *Fiddler on the Roof* reads: 'Act I — Prologue — Tradition: scene 1 — Kitchen of Tevye's House; scene 2 — Exterior of Tevye's House' and so on. On the other hand the setting for Higgins' study in *My Fair Lady* describes the room and its contents in a mass of detail. Whether this is an advantage is a matter of opinion for, as Curtis Canfield points out in *The Craft of Play Directing*, '. . . in too many cases, the more dogmatic a playwright is about how he wants the setting to look the more incomprehensible and ineffectual are his ideas likely to be when translated into terms of acting areas, sight-lines, and architectural realities.'

ACTING EDITIONS usually show the ground plans of the London settings. They are rarely to scale and are not as useful as may be at first thought. They were planned for a stage which is unlikely to conform in size, shape or proportions to that on which you will be performing, nor will the sight-lines match those of your venue, and you are unlikely to have all the technical aids of a West End theatre at your disposal.

From his constant readings of the script, the director will form an idea of the essential elements of each setting, the main entrances, the chief pieces of furniture required in the interior scenes; the geography of the exterior locales and the acting areas needed to accommodate his ensembles and dances. From these facts he can build up a picture of how each scene should appear and communicate these ideas to his designer.

However, it has to be admitted that in the majority of amateur musical productions, designers are the exception rather than the rule. In over 150 productions I have only twice had the services of one, and usually the scenery has to be hired.

Hiring scenery

Scenic contractors specialising in musical shows publish lists of titles for which they carry sets. These are generally copies of the original professional production's designs and will normally follow the ground-plans as published at the back of Acting Editions of the libretti. Sets come in three sizes: 18 ft high for the full-size stages and 16 ft or 12 ft for the smaller halls. (Scenic contractors have not yet gone metric.) Bear in mind that scenery is large and expensive to construct and store and contractors have to hold a large stock to cover all the demands made upon them. It is therefore natural that they use a set or cloth to cover more than one show. I once used a cloth for Richelieu's Palace in *The Three Musketeers* only to find it turn up again, at the same theatre, with the same company, as the corridor scene in *Call Me Madam*.

It pays to build up a personal knowledge of the stocks of various contractors. A wise director will also note any settings in other's productions that impress him and file details of the scenic supplier, whose name will appear in the programme, for future reference. In this way he will get to know the style and standard of various studios. Thus he finds that Messrs A paints in analine dyes, and his backcloths tend to be translucent – ideal for back lighting, but tending to let light bleed through when used for half stage sets. On the other hand Messrs B fails to keep his sets in good order, the flats show a tendency to warp and very often retouching of the paintwork is necessary.

In addition to the scenic contractors there are some professional theatres who are prepared to hire out scenery. Occasionally an amateur will commission new sets for a show which they will subsequently sell or hire. The pages of *NODA News* are the place to scan for these details.

Whenever hiring scenery write for a quotation. Do not limit your inquiry to one house since, if the show is a popular choice that season, sets may not be available on the dates that you require them.

When writing give the name of the company, the title of the show, the theatre or hall where the performances will be held, the dates of the performance, the day you require delivery of the sets and the height of the flats required.

In return you should receive a quotation for the hire, the cost of carriage plus, of course, VAT, and a set of ground-plans, normally drawn to scale of $\frac{1}{4}$ in. or $\frac{1}{2}$ in. to 1 ft (again, rarely metric). Study these plots in relation to your own ideas and the facilities of the hall or theatre. Impose them over your scaled plans of the stage (be certain that both are to the same scale) and see whether they fit. Check that lines are available, in the correct positions, for the cloths, borders and trailers, remembering to allow room for your electrical equipment. Consider whether the entrances are in the right positions and are easily accessible – some stages can have devilishly awkward corners; are they wide enough to allow easy passage of the players and any large properties which have to be taken on stage during the course of the action? Give thought too to the ease of setting, striking and the storage of the scenery when not in use for you do not want the wing space to be so cluttered that the actors cannot reach the stage. A great deal of preliminary work must be done before the scenic plots can be finalised and I have rarely used the sets exactly as they appeared in the original plans submitted by the contractors. Even in the older musical comedies, staged in three acts, with ample time to make scene changes in the intervals, some adaptation was generally necessary. Here is a practical example from *The Gipsy Baron*, Act 3, played at a town hall theatre.

The original design was symmetrical and extended the full depth of the stage; by the time that furniture was imposed on the design there was very little stage area for the ensemble and the dancers who had to perform a classical ballet.

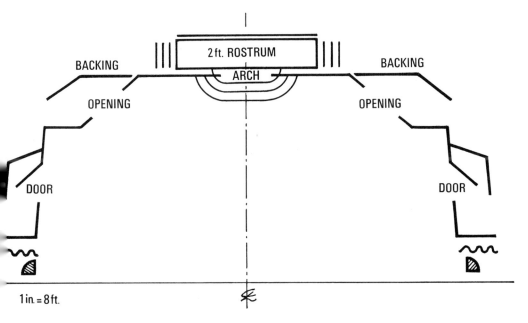

Fig. 1 *The Gipsy Baron*, Act 3: the scenic contractor's original plot

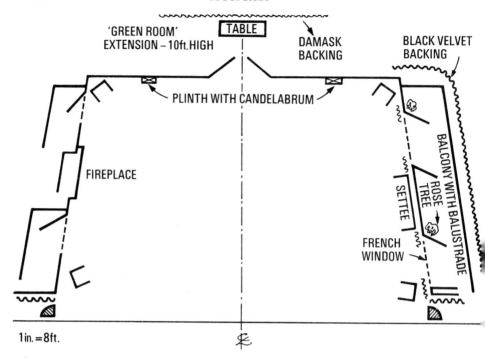

'GREEN ROOM'
EXTENSION – 10ft. HIGH

TABLE

DAMASK
BACKING

BLACK VELVET
BACKING

PLINTH WITH CANDELABRUM

FIREPLACE

BALCONY WITH BALUSTRADE

SETTEE

ROSE
TREE

FRENCH
WINDOW

1 in. = 8ft.

Fig. 2 *The Gipsy Baron*, Act 3: revised setting for a town hall stage

At this hall, the back of the stage contains a set of folding doors
running the full width of the back wall and giving onto a smaller hall
some 10 ft high. The height of the double doors in this contractor's sets
were only 8 ft high. We came up with the idea of setting as far back as
we could, using the smaller hall as the backing to the double doors
centre. This gave us an additional 4 ft in depth. The set was then
squared up and all the other exits confined to the OP side, above and
below a fireplace.

On the prompt side we added two sets of french windows giving onto
a balcony and, rather than use book wings to mask on this side, installed
a run of black velvet drapes (the scene was interior night) to give the
effect of a night sky outside. Several of the cast, when not required on
the main acting area, dressed the stage in groups on the balcony. The
effect, which was architecturally correct, gave the impression of a first-
floor salon of large proportions and provided ample acting space,
although certain entrances and exits had to be adjusted from the printed
libretto.

It is in the modern musicals, with their multiplicity of sets, one often flowing into the next without any break in the performance, that the ingenuity of the director will be stretched. *The Music Man* calls for 18 scenes made up of 13 different locales, which, on a stage offering little depth and no facilities for flying, is virtually impossible. However, after close study of the script and much discussion, I concluded that it could be played in 16 scenes using only seven locales. Briefly, this was effected by using two permanent archways, DL and DR, which served as the various porches and doorways called for in the script.

A single backcloth, largely hidden by 'house flats' doubled for the city centre of River City, Iowa, and, when clearly in view, for the bridge and Ice Cream Sociable scenes. The Paroo house was a small inset scene with the piano off-stage (as in a study or studio adjoining the set). The Gymnasium cloth, which had to be tumbled, doubled for the High School final scene, while the Library cloth, also tumbled, had to share the same set of lines as one of borders. Several scenes were dovetailed together and 'played in one'.

These were extreme measures for a difficult venue but they allowed us to play the show continuously and, as the printed synopsis states 'immediately following' for most scenes, I am sure that we did our best to carry out the author's intentions.

Scenes can often be combined without detriment to the show. The second act of *Pink Champagne* (the amateur version of *Die Fledermaus*) calls for a full-stage ballroom set, a front cloth Orangerie followed by a repeat of the ballroom. One can easily play this act 'in one'. The addition of a couple of lines to take the company off 'to supper' enables one to continue into the Orangerie scene and, later, the ensemble return from supper to go straight into the finale. By omitting the scene change, a more lavish setting can be designed for act two.

There are ways of making the set look bigger. Exteriors can often benefit by using a plain, well-lit sky cloth and a ground row, rather than a detailed landscape cloth which tends to bring the background forward. Wings can be set wider than the proscenium opening – I know that part will not be visible to some sections of the audience, but unless some vital action has to take place near a wing, what does it matter? If height allows, rostra can be used, allowing the ensemble to be ranged at varying levels.

Having established that the director of amateur musicals will, in most cases, have to design or adapt his scenery, it is pertinent to suggest that he should have a basic knowledge of the construction and handling of scenery.

Scenery may be described as being either two- or three-dimensional. As the description implies, two-dimensional scenery is flat although sometimes several units may be assembled to make a three-dimensional form on the stage. Two-dimensional scenery can be further classified as being framed or unframed and together these groups will account for the majority of scenery used in a musical production – embodying the cloths, borders, legs, flats, wings and stage draperies. The term three-dimensional scenery is self-explanatory and includes all the solid forms used – rostra, pillars, staircases, rocks, tree stumps and the like. Today a fair amount of builder's scaffolding is used in sets and this would come under the heading of three-dimensional scenery in this context. All the aforementioned items may be subdivided into practical and non-practical pieces. Staircases and rostra are examples of practical weightbearing solids, whilst decorative pillars can be termed non-weightbearing.

It does not fall within the scope of this book to discuss the various methods of constructing and handling scenery. There are many excellent books on the subject and the aspiring director is referred to these. He should familiarise himself with the various scene-changing techniques; the comparative advantages and disadvantages of the pin-and-rail (or hemp) and counter-weight systems of flying; bridling, breasting, tripping and tumbling techniques as well as the uses and functions of tracked and pivoted trucks, revolving stages, lift or elevator stages and the uses of various traps.

A word about sight-lines

These are the audience's lines of visibility and determine how much of the stage is in view. They can be easily determined mathematically using a sheet of graph paper, a ruler and a plan and elevation of the theatre. The horizontal sight-lines are drawn from the outermost seats on the left and right of the house where the audience can be seated. Where the seating arrangements are widely flared, the audience seating on the extreme right of the auditorium will see very little of the prompt (stage left) side of the stage and vice versa.

The vertical sight-lines are harder to plot since there is seldom a sectional drawing of the theatre readily available, and they are most difficult when the auditorium comprises one or more balconies.

The pattern of these sight-lines will determine the shape of the set and the acting area where any action will be in full view from all parts of the theatre. It may sometimes be necessary for some of the ensemble to

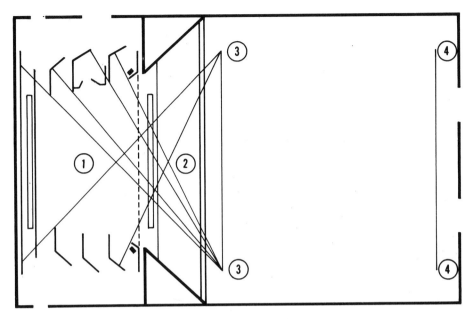

Fig. 3   Horizontal sight-lines

Key: 1, Stage; 2, Orchestra Pit. Sight-lines are checked from the end seats of: 3, Front row of stalls; 4, Back row of stalls; 5, Front row of any circle; and 6, Back row of any circle. Sight-lines from any existing boxes should also be checked

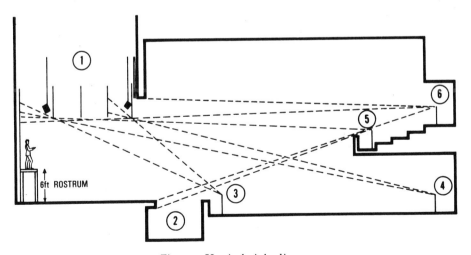

Fig. 4   Vertical sight-lines

be hidden from the audience's view but the principal players should always be positioned well within the acting area.

The final scenic plot

The revised settings should be drawn up to scale, fully detailed and returned to the scenic contractor for his comments. If at all possible make an appointment to see them (N.B. — always make an appointment) to discuss and adjust your ideas. Such meetings are of immense value and I have found that an hour spent with the hirers will result in the whole matter being resolved to both parties' satisfaction. Moreover one can usually see specimen flats and get an indication of colour schemes, which is of special benefit when it comes to selecting furniture and fittings for the interior sets.

One should note that some suppliers send out their backcloths unbattened and it's worth making sure at this stage whether you will need to supply lengths of battening when it comes to the 'get in'. In addition, many will include certain properties with the scenery. This is often done as a matter of course but not all firms indicate just exactly what they will supply and one can end up in needless expense. The roundabout in *Carousel* and the surrey in *Oklahoma!* are obvious items in this category, but not so obvious are the player piano plus piano stool in *The Music Man*, the trick knife board in *The Pajama Game* and such mundane items as tree stumps, rustic tables and benches. It is always well worth establishing exactly what the contractor can supply and detail the items on the finalised plot. Copies of the agreed plots are sent to the supplying company, the stage manager, the lighting designer (if there is one), director and choreographer. The last two can then set to work on preparing the prompt book and the dance routines with full knowledge of the dimensions and limitations of the sets.

Making your own scenery

Whether it is the increasing cost of musicals or that more schools are becoming involved in mounting them, many groups are making their own scenery these days. Schools are especially well equipped to handle such an exercise with their workshops and teachers, for it takes time, space and a lot of equipment and expertise to create good sets. Nevertheless I have seen some excellent examples of 'home-made' work: an *Oklahoma!* by a Yeovil school, a superb set of designs for *Lucia di*

Lammermoor by a north London technical college, an impressive *Cabaret* and an *Orpheus in the Underworld* by two local operatic societies. In addition I have noted reports of projected scenery being used to good effect in *Brigadoon* and an exciting production, in the round, of *West Side Story*. Having experienced the thrill of conceiving a show from scratch with the London amateur première of *The Wizard of Oz*, I know how exciting it can be to have a show designed to one's particular needs and although such a venture is rarely cheaper than hiring the sets, the rewards are infinitely greater.

Performing in the round

The very nature of musicals precludes most from being staged in the round, although the recent successful production of *Cats* has illustrated that some can be mounted in this way — *Cats* was more a thrust production since it did boast a huge backcloth backing the set.

An arena stage imposes very strict discipline on the director, set, and lighting designer, and unless a show has been specifically composed for arena production, a great deal of preliminary thought must take place before embarking on such a project. Such scenery as is used must be confined to low units or skeleton pieces that can be seen through. Design details become very important because of the nearness of the audience and the lack of larger elements of scenery in the composition.

The basic number of lanterns required to light each acting area will be doubled and great care must be employed in focusing and directing these in order not to dazzle the audience, whilst still illuminating the actors. Generally the rules laid down in the chapter on lighting will apply, but one must bear in mind that the effect of any particular lantern will vary, depending from where it is viewed. What appears flat frontal lighting in one part of the theatre, could easily be a dazzling beam of back lighting when seen from the other side of the arena stage.

Equipment will, of necessity, be placed overhead — over the arena itself and above the surrounding audience. Since fewer lanterns are normally used, and they illuminate from varying angles with less overlap of beams than on the proscenium stage, colour needs to be used with great subtlety. One major problem is the location of the orchestra, and the means by which the conductor will control the singers. The director will need to accept that there will always be some members of the cast who have their backs to part of the audience and also the conductor, wherever he is placed.

An alternative to the arena stage, and one which has been successfully proven for school productions, is a combination of the school stage with a thrust stage, on ground-level in front. The two levels are connected by a series of graduated platforms, steps or ramps. The audience sits around the thrust area which is used mainly for the dances and ensembles where one wishes to use larger numbers than can be accommodated on the stage itself.

The orchestra is situated to one side of the hall from which the musical director can see and control the company. Large set pieces can be used on the stage, the stage curtains being closed to cover any scene changes. Smaller, free-standing pieces may be used on the thrust area.

One will need lighting to cover the thrust area, similar to that already described for the arena stage, in addition to the normal proscenium stage lighting.

Apart from the conventional stage entrances, one can, if the layout of the building permits, make entrances and exits through the audience. A variation is to build a second platform at the opposite end of the hall to the stage and connect the two with a raised acting area. In this case the audience is split and sits along both sides of the hall.

With all this choice of layouts, the amateur has one big advantage over the professional. The halls in which so many amateurs perform do not have fixed seating, and any variation in the seating plan is easily accomplished. Imagine the time and cost of reseating the New London Theatre for *Cats*!

[4]

Blocking the show

Every show needs a prompt book. It is the director's most essential tool and the preparation of it is one of his most arduous chores. There are wide differences of opinion about what the book should contain and when it should be prepared. Some directors block the show 'on the floor' with the actors, devoting their pre-rehearsal time with the consideration of such weighty matters as the inner meaning of the script, the nature of the characters and the subtle interplay of their motives. At the other extreme are those who quietly and conscientiously block the show in private, before rehearsals begin, and sometimes before the cast is selected. It may be argued that they cannot take into account the personalities and individual playing styles of the actors who will eventually play the parts, but I would counter this with Curtis Canfield's remark in *The Craft of Play Directing* that 'moves are blocked for characters, not for actors'. In other words, when a director is preparing his book before rehearsals, the moves he plots should be determined by his understanding of the characters found in the text, not by the personality of the artist playing the role. It is Billy Bigelow crossing down stage left, not Joe Bloggs, or whoever is acting the part.

George Bernard Shaw had no doubts about when to block: 'If, before you begin rehearsing, you sit down to the manuscript of your play and work out all the stage business . . . then you will at the first rehearsal get a command of the production that nothing will shake afterwards.'

For my own part, I consider that the prompt book should be the director's and stage manager's vade-mecum. In it should be found all the actors' entrances and exits, all the moves and details of any stage business, the cuts, pauses, notes on inflections, pace, speech rhythms, together with all music, lighting, effects and curtain cues. In short, it should contain all the information that is needed to show how the piece will be staged and, certainly in the early stages of directing, I would recommend that as much detail as possible be included and that basic blocking is plotted before going into rehearsal. This will give the director a base from which to start. During rehearsals he will alter, correct and refine his original ideas; sometimes an idea which looked good on paper just will not work on the floor, and the scene may have to be rethought. Few sensible directors will regard their initial blocking as sacrosanct.

What then of the published Acting Editions? As I have already remarked, these are very often based on the original professional production with all that that implies. By all means use them as a reference, but a good director will always plan his production for himself.

All this information must be incorporated into both the libretto and score. The neatest and most accessible form is to have these volumes interleaved with blank sheets and rebound by a bookbinder. (In 1982 the cost of this service was around £12.00.) This outlay is fully justified, as both books will undergo severe handling during the weeks of preparation and rehearsal.

Do not be tempted to work from the libretto alone. This is a false economy. The score is essential; apart from the music one can see the number of bars and the tempo of the music available for business and moves in the vocal items (which are often abbreviated in the libretto), the melos, music under dialogue, dances and scene changes.

In recent years, the copyright owners of some modern musicals have not issued printed libretti. Instead they hire out a small number of stencilled copies which have to be returned, unmarked, after use. This creates difficulties for the director since, should he decide to photocopy, he could be infringing the copyright. It might be argued that, since this copy was for his own use, the action came under the heading of 'fair dealing' but I feel that the safer course is to interleave the pages of the script with blank sheets in a loose-leaf binder — one of the type which have a spring back to hold the sheets. All markings would have to be made on the blank sheets and the script returned after use.

Editing the text

In law, the words and music are the property of the copyright holders. They may not be cut or altered without permission, but the owners are generally most understanding and ready to help the amateur and I have never been refused permission to make such amendments as I found necessary for technical or physical reasons. Indeed, some go so far as to indicate cuts and alterations in their printed libretti and scores — for example, French's *Bitter Sweet* and Weinberger's *Gipsy Baron*.

It is advisable to keep the playing time of most musicals to about two and a half hours, including any intervals. If one is in the habit of playing two houses – late matinée and evening performance – on Saturdays, the production must be tailored to these. A very rough yardstick to gauge the running time of a show is to allow two minutes per printed page of the libretto – it invariably works. In a few of the older shows running times are indicated in the script – that for *The New Moon* gives an average playing time of 3 hours 4¾ minutes!

Apart from keeping the performance to a reasonable length, one must also consider editing lines which have ceased to have their original meaning, or which evoke wrong audience response.

Cuts may also be made for practical reasons. In *Charlie Girl* Lady Hadwell enters on a tricycle. Apart from obtaining a suitable machine, there are problems of stage and wing space to consider and if these cannot be resolved the only thing to do is to cut the tricycle and amend the lines accordingly. In the same show a motorcycle is essential to the plot. In this case, if a machine cannot be accommodated one may have to consider doing another show.

Additions are sometimes possible. A solo for Sergeant Meryll has long been omitted from the vocal score of *The Yeomen of the Guard*. If one has a good baritone playing the role (and Meryll has no solos) it is worth reinstating 'A Laughing Boy But Yesterday' for the satisfaction of the singer and the delight of the audience.

The Gilbert and Sullivan Operas are out of copyright and new, non-traditional productions can be mounted. Three notable professional productions have been *The Black Mikado*, the Canadian version of *HMS Pinafore* and the New York production of *The Pirates of Penzance*. It can only be hoped that such productions will encourage societies and directors to see the Savoy Operas in a new light. While mourning the demise of the D'Oyly Carte Company, I deplored their habit of giving all the traditional encores whether or not the audience response warranted. Encores must be planned and rehearsed but only given if demanded by the applause; in general I am a firm believer in the old adage: 'Always leave them wanting more.'

Cuts, alterations and encores should be made only after a great deal of thought, and in consultation with the musical director and the choreographer when they affect the singing or the dancing. They should be made before the first read-through to avoid disappointment amongst the cast who might otherwise feel that their parts are being unreasonably shortened. If necessary, explain to them why you have made the cuts and how your editing will benefit the show as a whole.

Preparing the prompt book

The director's first step in staging a production is to visualise it in space. With the aid of the script and his imagination, he must see an action 'involving people with other people and with the world they live in. If the actors were left to themselves, they would get in front of one another and muddle the composition, and each would move without regard to what the others were doing. The grouping would be meaningless, and the attention of the audience would be scattered' (George and Portia Kernodle, *Invitation to the Theatre*).

To assist him in this period of imaginative experimentation, the more ambitious director may prepare scale models of his settings, or use rough sketches, similar to a film or television story board. I find that scale plans of the sets with counters, golf tees or chessmen to represent the individual characters, serve for experiment.

Stage directions are always given from the actor's point of view. The part of the stage furthest from the audience is termed upstage, that nearest them, downstage; these terms stemming from the days when most stages had a rake.

To assist in directing the actor's moves the stage floor is divided into nine designated areas (Fig. 5):

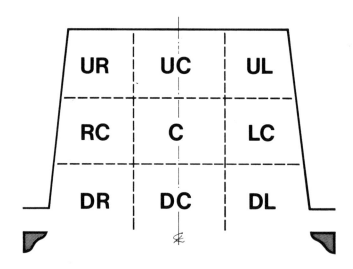

Fig. 5   The main areas of the stage

There are four further subdivisions around the centre area – Up Left Centre and Down Left Centre; Up Right Centre and Down Right Centre and three others for the back wall – Centre Back and Left and Right Centre Back. All these terms are abbreviated to initials when writing.

Movement around an object on the stage again makes illusion to the old sloping stage. An actor is not told to 'go behind' a table or 'in front' of a chair, but to 'go above' or 'below' the object.

The most dominant position on the stage is generally taken to be DC whilst those areas UL and UR are considered particularly good for scenes requiring 'soft', lyrical or brooding moods.

French scenes

Before blocking a show go through the libretto and underline all the directions and stage business in red ink. Any cuts or alterations are noted and any vocal items or dialogue over music struck out and cross referenced to the appropriate page in the score.

Then consider the libretto in terms of 'French scenes'. These small segments are the director's work units and are usually determined by the entry or exit of a character. Here is an example from *Fiddler on the Roof*, Act I scene I:

(1) From the opening until Yente enters.
(2) Dialogue between Yente, Motel and Golde, ending with Yente's exit.
(3) From Yente's exit to end of scene, including the number.

While experimenting with the moves for these sequences, the following basic rules are observed:

(1) Generally speaking, actors should move only on their own lines.
(2) A speaking actor should cross downstage of a silent actor.
(3) A moving actor attracts the attention, provided he contrasts others who are static.
(4) Whenever possible, lines should be spoken within the confines of the proscenium arch. As soon as one addresses lines above the stage opening, the carrying power of the voice will drop by as much as 60% and the voice must be raised to compensate for this loss.
(5) No move should be made without a purpose. Among the reasons for moving may be listed: practicability, emphasis, emotion, proportion or balance, character relationships.

(6) Wherever possible, an actor leaving a scene should be placed conveniently near an exit to enable him to deliver his line and depart.

A practical example of blocking principal moves

Let us now take a short sequence from *Pink Champagne* and block it together. This is the scene as it appears on pages 17 and 18 in French's Acting Edition:

ROSALINDA (*To herself*) Poor Gabriel! I must say he shows courage – he's going to prison with his head held high. I love him for that. (*With a change of mood*) No, I *don't* love him, I *detest* him! Whatever happens, I'll *never* forgive him for last night! (*With resolution she moves up R to windows, and turns up the lamp. Then she crosses L to the console table and waits.*)
Off stage there is a great noise as Alfred scales the balcony. The music fades out.
(*Running to the window*) Ssh!
Alfred appears at balcony.

ALFRED (*Fulsomely*) My beloved!

ROSALINDA (*Moving C*) Be careful, do – the flower pots!
There is a crash of flower pots off stage. Alfred enters and looks around possessively.
(*Reproachfully*) Alfred – my husband!

ALFRED Why worry about *him*? He's on his way to prison. (*He moves down to R of Rosalinda*).

ROSALINDA You *know* about it?

ALFRED (*With satisfaction*) Of course. It's in every newspaper and a picture of the Bat! (*He kneels and takes her hand*) How an angel like you could have married such a hooligan!

ROSALINDA (*Pathetically, mopping her eye with her handkerchief*) He *has* been rather – *unkind*!

ALFRED (*Rising and crossing L to the table*) Unkind? His behaviour has been monstrous. (*Eyeing the table greedily*) Not *supper*?

ROSALINDA I thought perhaps a glass of wine . . .

ALFRED (*Moving to L of the sofa*) You think of everything. A dressing-gown – a smoking cap. And to think how nervous I was of being alone with my goddess for the first

	time . . .'. (*He removes his jacket*) I never expected to be made at home like this!
ROSALINDA	(*Astonished*) Whatever are you doing?
ALFRED	What seems the most natural thing in the world. I'm taking over the duties of the profligate! (*He puts on the dressing-gown*)
ROSALINDA	His d-d-duties . . .?
ALFRED	You'll be surprised how naturally I slip into them!
ROSALINDA	(*With raised eyebrows*) Surprised is hardly the word!
ALFRED	(*Putting on the smoking cap*) Now what about a little supper, darling wife? (*He moves to the chair above the table L and sits*)
ROSALINDA	(*Doubtfully*) Darling *wife*?
ALFRED	(*Inspecting the tray*) Foie gras – a cold capon – and a bottle of pink champagne. Delicious! (*He picks up the champagne bottle*) I have to be rather particular what I eat.
ROSALINDA	(*Nettled*) Oh, you *do*, do you?
ALFRED	My voice, you know. (*He sings a scale*) Now, as for breakfast . . .
ROSALINDA	(*Horrified*) Breakfast?
ALFRED	Love gives one the appetite of a god. All the same I must be careful. Just some lightly boiled eggs – a dish of sweetbreads – a little fish – a slice of ham – a toasted roll or two . . . (*He unfastens the champagne bottle*)
ROSALINDA	(*Cutting in*) Don't imagine that you're going to breakfast *here*!
ALFRED	You would rather go out, my love?
ROSALINDA	(*Sweeping agitatedly upstage and then down*) You'll be going out – and long before breakfast, too! Do you want to destroy my reputation entirely?
ALFRED	(*Aside, opening the bottle*) I can see that I have been a little impetuous. I should have let things take their course. (*Aloud*) Do not worry, Rosalinda mine. (*He rises and, moving to R of the table, pours out two glasses of pink champagne.*) The night is still young, let us live for the moment, let us say that I am here just to take a glass of wine with you and *sing*?
ROSALINDA	No, no, not *that*!
ALFRED	(*Petulantly*) Not sing? But you used to like my voice?
ROSALINDA	Unfortunately I liked it too much, but tonight . . .

ALFRED   *(Trying to embrace her)* My angel! Come to my arms. This
                 is the moment of which your foolish, adoring Alfred has
                 always dreamed!

ROSALINDA *(Escaping hastily down* R) I think perhaps you had better
                 sing after all!

This scene presents several problems. There is a lot of business with
the food, champagne and the glasses, as well as the changing into the
dressing-gown. The first problem to resolve is the placing of these
important properties, so let us refresh our memory by looking again at
the general setting (Fig. 6):

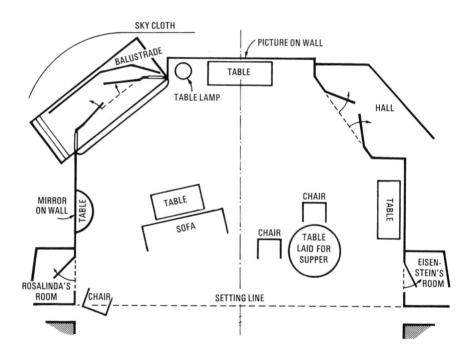

Fig. 6 *Pink Champagne*, Act I: plan of the set

The lantern, which is alight, stands on the small table above the
French windows UR. The dressing-gown (Eisenstein's) is draped over
the back of the sofa DC and the smoking cap is on the sofa towards the
right end. The supper has already been laid on table DLC; the placing of
the food, cutlery and crockery, is extremely critical if the scene is to play
smoothly (Fig. 7):

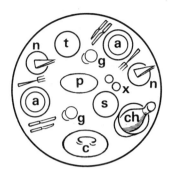

a   Place setting of 2 plates,
    2 knives and 1 fork
c   Chicken on covered salver
ch Champagne, unopened in cooler
g   Wine glasses
n   Napkins on side plates
p   Dish of pâté
s   Bowl of salad
t   Plate of toast
x   Condiments

Fig. 7   *Pink Champagne*, Act 1: details of the setting of the supper table

The scene starts as Eisenstein leaves, by the double doors UL, supposedly to go to jail. Adele, the maid, leaves at the same time, closing the doors behind her. Rosalinda is DR, gazing after her departing husband (Fig. 8):

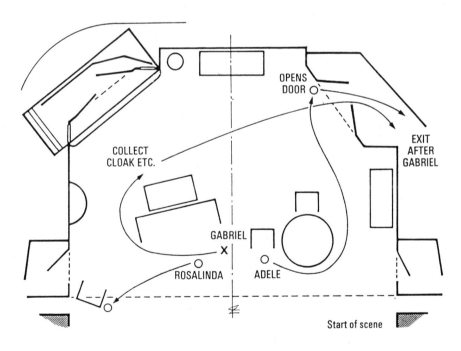

Fig. 8   *Pink Champagne*, Act 1: positions at start of scene

She turns downstage as she speaks. She is in love with her husband, despite his antics of the previous night and a smile would not be out of place here, and if she holds her hands lightly clasped to her chin, she can make a strong gesture here.

ROSALINDA (*To herself*) Poo Gabriel! I must say he shows courag — he's going to prison with his head held high. I love him for that.

She is in a bad position from which to move to the lamp. She can reinforce her anger with a move — x to table DRC. She looks at the supper for two and this gives her an idea. x above sofa to lamp she waves it as a signal. Replaces it. Suddenly a pang of conscience, she breaks away to R back of sofa (Fig. 9)

(*With a change of mood*) No, I *don't* lov him, I *detest him*! Whatever happens I'll *never* forgive him for last night! (*With resolution she moves up R to th windows*)

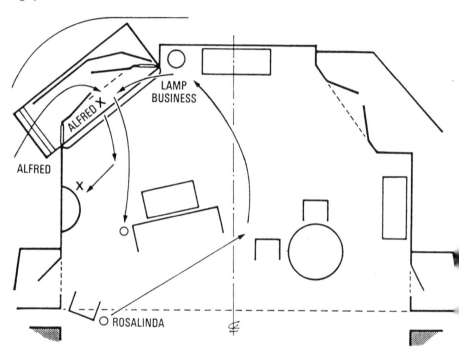

Fig. 9   *Pink Champagne*, Act I: blocking the principles' moves

Alfred is presumably using a creeper to assist his climb to the balcony, and the noise he creates will be of cracking twigs and of his physical exertions. These hardly give rise to a great noise as indicated. Moreover, if Alfred appears on the balcony before giving his line, he will not be seen by a large part of the audience. I decided therefore to bring forward Alfred's 'My beloved!' and let him shout this from off stage. The book now reads:

Off stage there is a great noise as Alfre scales the balcony.
ROSALINDA (*Running to the window* Ssh!
ALFRED   My beloved!

She must also look down as the room is supposed to be on the first floor! She places a warning finger to her lips. As he climbs over the balcony Rosalinda can back into the room, and, as Alfred's foot is obviously going straight into her potted geraniums:

Alfred can swear sotto voce 'Damn!'

Having recovered his composure, Alfred makes a very theatrical entrance, arms extended as if to take Rosalinda in an embrace. She turns away to DRC, teasing him.

To underline the fact that Alfred is an egotist and very vain, I altered the suggested move and instead let Alfred go to the mirror on the wall R and admire himself.

Slightly taken aback by his knowledge. Since he is looking away from her he cannot see her concern. Again I have altered the move. Instead of kneeling, he turns to her.

She searches for a suitable word.

Alfred takes her literally X to her. This brings him in direct line with the supper table. Instead of consoling Rosalinda as she anticipates, he continues his X and his speech (Fig. 10, p. 44):

Rosalinda can show her pique with a break R. This also serves to clear the sofa for the next sequence. Alfred now turns to reply and in so doing, sees the dressing-gown and smoking cap.

Off stage UR there is a great noise as Alfred scales the balcony
(*Off UR in loud stage whisper*) My beloved!
ROSALINDA (*Quickly running to window UR and looking off*) Ssh!

Alfred appears on the balcony

ROSALINDA Be careful, do – the flower pots!

There is a crash of flower pots off stage, UR. Alfred enters.

ROSALINDA (*Reproachfully*) Alfred – my husband!

ALFRED Why worry about *him*? He's on his way to prison.

ROSALINDA You *know* about it?
ALFRED (*With satisfaction*) Of course. It's in every newspaper, and a picture of the Bat! How an angel like you could have married such a hooligan!

ROSALINDA He *has* been rather – *unkind*!

ALFRED Unkind! His behaviour has been monstrous.

Not *supper*?

ROSALINDA (*Breaks R*) I thought perhaps a glass of wine . . .

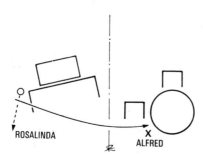

Fig. 10

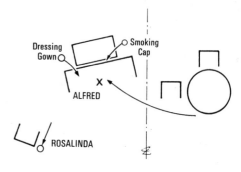

Fig. 11

ALFRED (*Turning to her*) You think
of *everything*. A dressing-gown —
smoking cap.

Here he starts to remove his jacket (Fig. 11.)

And to think how nervous I was o
being alone with my goddess for the
first time . . . I never expected to be
made at home like this!

*He lays his jacket over the L end of the sofa.
Rosalinda, not knowing what he intends, is
astonished and X to C.*

ROSALINDA (*Astonished*) Whatever
are you doing?
ALFRED What seems the most
natural thing in the world. I'm
taking over the duties of that prof-
ligate!
ROSALINDA His d-d-duties . . .?

*You will notice that the Acting Edition makes
Alfred don the dressing-gown on his line 'I'm
taking over the duties . . .' I found his next speech
matched the business to the lines and substituted
the move accordingly. He puts on the dressing-
gown.*

ALFRED You'll be surprised how
naturally I slip into them!

*Alfred must not register Rosalinda's next line,
and is engaged in tying the cord of the dressing-
gown. Rosalinda is afraid that matters are going
too far! She widens the gap between Alfred and
herself by moving to the chair DR. She can also use
this for support.*

*This invariably gets a laugh and his line should
be held.*

ROSALINDA (*With raised eyebrows*)
Surprised is hardly the word!
ALFRED (*Putting on smoking cap*)

If necessary he can study the contents of the table.

The Acting Edition makes Alfred sit here, but I prefer to keep him standing for greater mobility. Things are certainly getting out of hand! Here, as already noted, the food must be in pre-planned positions. The capon is under a dish cover, and has some edible portions laid by.

Now how about a little supper darling wife?

ROSALINDA (*Doubtfully*) Darling wife?

ALFRED (*Inspecting the table; Foie gras* – a cold capon – (he picks at it) – *picking up champagne bottle from the cooler*) and a bottle of pink champagne. Delicious. I have to be rather particular what I eat.

ROSALINDA Oh, you *do*, do you?

ALFRED My voice you know. (*He sings a scale.*)

Over his shoulder, inspecting the bottle. Rosalinda is now fuming and her manner changes to an icy tone. It is amusing if Alfred can run his 'Now as for breakfast' on from the end of his vocalising. He must be prepared to complete this sentence. Rosalinda really cuts in.

Now, as for breakfast . . .

ROSALINDA Breakfast?

Turning to her for once.

ALFRED Love gives one the appetite of a god. All the same I must be careful. Just some lightly boiled eggs – a dish of sweetbreads – a little fish – a slice of ham – a toasted roll or two . . .

He starts to unfasten the foil covering of the champagne bottle.

It is a good plan to accelerate as Alfred runs though the list.

ROSALINDA (*Cutting in*) Don't imagine that you're going to breakfast *here*.

ALFRED You would rather go out, my love?

Very annoyed now, and she sweeps upstage R. Alfred engrossed with the cork tosses his reply over his shoulder. Rosalinda makes a strong angry move to him.

ROSALINDA (X *to Alfred*) You'll be going out – and long before breakfast, too! (X *below sofa to* DR.) Do you want to destroy my reputation entirely?

Here again I have altered the moves suggested by the Acting Edition. Alfred has at last been made aware of Rosalinda's disturbed frame of mind. She stands DR *her back to him, her finger drumming angrily on the back of the seat. He has been halted in his business of opening the bottle.*

ALFRED (*Aside, front*) I can see that
I have been a little impetuous. I
should have let things take their
course.

He opens the bottle with a 'pop'.

Returns bottle to the cooler.

He ends on a wide appeal.
Rosalinda turns sharply.

(*Aloud*) Do not worry, Rosalinda
mine.
(*He pours two glasses of champagne*). The
night is still young, let us live for the
moment. Let us say that I am here
just to take a glass of wine with you
(turns DL) and *sing*.

ROSALINDA No, no, not *that*!
ALFRED (*Petulantly*) Not sing! But
you used to like my voice?
ROSALINDA Unfortunately I liked

She turns away R.

it too much, but tonight . . .
ALFRED (X, *trying to embrace her*) My
angel! Come to my arms. This is the
moment of which your foolish, ador-
ing Alfred has always dreamed!
ROSALINDA (*Quick X to DL. Below
Alfred.*) I think perhaps you had
better *sing* after all!

I do not suggest that the interpretation given in this analysis is the
definitive one; it is quoted merely as an example of the mechanics of
blocking.

Blocking the chorus moves

Now to consider an example of ensemble blocking. I have selected a
number from *White Horse Inn*, the London amateur première of which I
directed at the now defunct Finsbury Park Empire. (The musical
number is No. 4, 'Arrival of Guests', which will be found on pages
27–35 in the vocal score.)

The show is played mainly in a standing set, depicting the exterior of
the White Horse Inn. The backcloth shows Lake Wolfgangsee with the
mountains in the distance. The inn occupies stage left; on the opposite
side stands the mayor's house.

During this vocal number, the guests arrive by the lake steamer and are greeted by the maids from the White Horse Inn, the porters from various local hotels, and Alpine guides and flower girls who are trying to sell their services and wares.

The first problem is the steamer. This is a built-up piece mounted on a truck, which is propelled across the back of the set at the appropriate time. Friends in Austria gave me details of the actual White Horse Inn and I was delighted to learn that the landing stage was quite a distance from the hotel. I decided therefore that it was both permissible and logical to let the steamer arrive, off stage, during the dialogue preceding the number. This gave extra stage space, which even at the Empire was at a premium, and allowed the electric ground rows an unobstructed throw onto the backcloth. The finalised ground plan for this show therefore became as in Fig. 12:

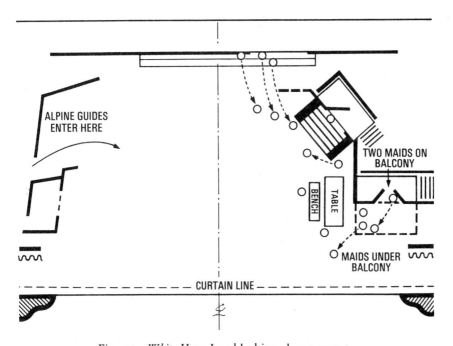

Fig. 12 *White Horse Inn*: blocking chorus moves

Turning to the score, we find that this number requires a double chorus – maids (sopranos), Alpine guides (first and second tenors), flower girls (first and second contralto) and porters (baritone and basses) as well as another chorus, comprising all these voices, to play the various guests.

The best voices should be chosen for the maids, guides, flower girls and porters, since these sections sing separately. At the same time the heights of these parts must be considered. Ideally we shall require at least:

10 Maids who should be petite.
  6 Alpine guides who should look like outdoor types (and have good knees as they wear lederhosen).
  6 Flower girls, who can be rather more buxom.
  7 Porters, who should be tall and commanding, plus Franz.

The rest of the chorus, say 18, can be of assorted voices and shapes, while in addition we must keep in reserve a bride and bridegroom who make a brief entrance at the end of the number.

The various groups are indicated as follows:

Maids	A, B, C, D, E, F, G, H, I, J.
Alpine guides	I, II, III, IV, V, VI.
Flower girls	a, b, c, d, e, f.
Porters	1, 2, 3, 4, 5, 6, 7 plus Franz.
Tourists	T

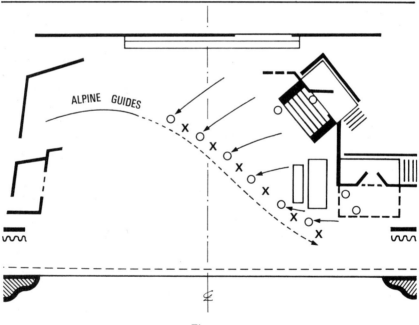

Fig. 13

Before the number starts, the maids have been told to clean up the inn. They all have matching dusters. There are two bars introduction which illustrate, rather well, the shaking of a duster. The same rhythm occurs in bars 7 and 8. So we start the number with the maids flicking their dusters and moving to position as indicated in Fig. 12. Whilst they sing they hold their dusters by the diagonal corners. On 'Heigh ho' they throw up their hands in mock despair, and at the end of their section (4 bars before fig. 2) go back to their dusting.

Now follow the Alpine guides, but if we let them enter as they sing, we shall lack volume and risk the chance of a bad vocal attack. So put their entrance back a little; the most suitable place is as the maids sing '. . . for a chambermaid'. Counting two steps per bar, this will get them eight steps on stage, in full view of the musical director before they have to sing. The music has a strong march beat and their entrance should have a swagger. Thumbs are thrust in braces and they sing lustily, attracting the maids who break off their work and come down to them (Fig. 13).

The flower girls have a gentler tune, and four bars of introduction. Their entrance can be far more leisurely. They carry baskets of flowers

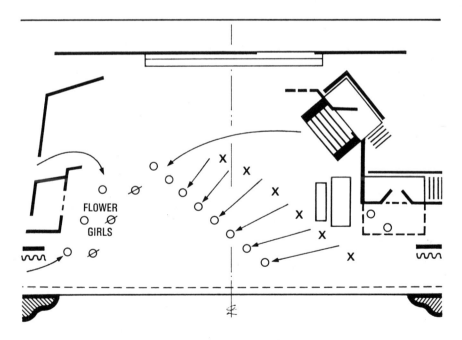

Fig. 14

and they group DR. The maids leave the men and cross to admire the blooms (Fig. 14).

Both the guides and the flower girls enter R which has been established as the direction of the village.

The porters have no introductory bars to their section and their entrance must be brought forward. They can enter severally and in a leisurely fashion, from both UR and UL (Fig. 15):

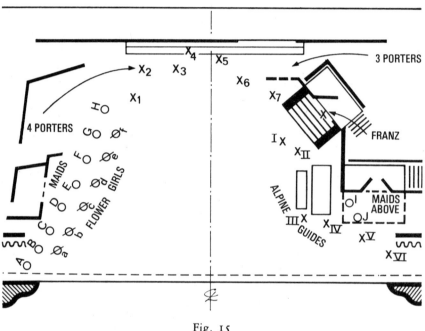

Fig. 15

At fig. 5 in the score, the counter melodies get complicated and it is advisable to keep the picture static and concentrate on the singing. After all, these characters have assembled to greet the guests, not to sell to each other. On the musical director's advice, I kept the voices in groups here.

At fig. 8 in the score, the guests arrive. This point is usually the cue for the rest of the chorus to burst onto the scene; but analyse this entrance. We have a collection of various ages, sexes and nationalities who have arrived at Wolfgang for a holiday. Some have been here before, and know their way around, others are strangers, temporarily lost, some are having language difficulties, and most are carrying luggage. So the entrances will vary in speed and character and the music from fig. 8 to one bar before fig. 10 can be utilised for this movement. As the guests enter, the maids, porters, guides, and flower girls mill around, seeking their clients, whilst the music grows to a crescendo. A scene of energetic turmoil. Here are the suggested moves as listed in my score; each is cued to a specific bar of music:

(1) Porter I meets two tourists, a man and a woman, and, with flower girls E, F, X DL to meet guide VI.
Lady stays with porter and guide, man with flower girls.

(2) Maids a, b, c, X to DLC.

(3) Porter 2 meets two tourists, man and woman; joined by guide I and all X DR. Man joins flower girls A, B.

(4) Two lady tourists enter X DLC. Meet maids a, b, c. Sit on cases.

(5) Porter 3 meets three lady tourists. Conducts them to LC where they are met by guide V.

(6) Porter 4 meets tourist lady, joined by guide II and they X RC.

(7) Two tourists X to Franz on steps of hotel.

(8) Porter 5 meets one tourist, conducts to ULC and met by guide IV.

(9) Flower girls CD meet two male tourists and take UC.

(10) Porter 6 and guide III meet female tourist and take URC.

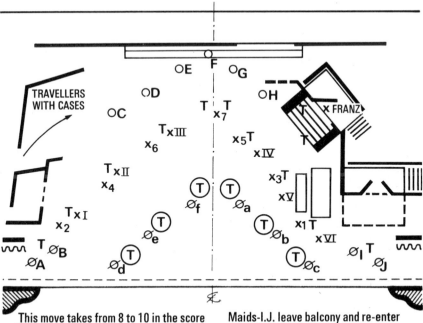

This move takes from 8 to 10 in the score
(T)= Travellers sit on cases

Maids-I.J. leave balcony and re-enter through arch below

Fig. 16

This looks very complicated, but rehearse it slowly and, with repetition, you will find that the moves flow quite naturally. It is essential to work out mass movements in detail like this, so that every member of the ensemble knows exactly what he or she should do (Fig. 16).

The picture should be held at fig. 10 in the score for the final repeat of the chorus, which is lusty. We could finish with this grouping, but a final move will underline the climax, so at the first bar on page 35, the seated characters rise on 'we raise our fees', pick up their cases on the 3rd bar 'and that's why you hear' and on bar 5 move to position as Fig. 17.

They halt in these positions on the last line, cases are placed on the floor and there is a general appeal.

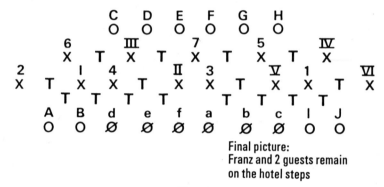

Fig. 17

One last point. The vocal line in the score ends on a short note, a quaver, and the orchestra continues with a strain from the 'Wedding March' to announce the arrival of the bride and groom. This music is usually drowned by the audience applause (or should be!) and the musical director and I therefore decided to make the last note 'year', a minim and give a pause mark to the note to round off the vocal portion with a good climax. The orchestra cut off completely until brought in by the musical director; the 'Wedding March' was easily heard and the allusion to the bride and groom, who entered here, was clearly made.

Dialogue over music

This can take a variety of forms. An easy example would be the dialogue of the Pirate King in the 'Paradox' trio in *The Pirates of Penzance*. Here, the words are intoned over a series of rising and descending chords and, provided the actor observes the punctuation and stresses the first word in each bar, there is no real difficulty until the last word, 'over'. This is vocalised and must be in strict tempo to allow a clean run into the duet with Ruth.

Another well-known example is the singing-speaking of Professor Higgins in *My Fair Lady* so expertly mastered by Rex Harrison (who made no claims to be a singer).

Far more difficult are the numbers in *The Music Man* for Harold Hill, whilst the Rock Island opening number is a headache for both actors and director. Comprising over 160 bars, this is a scene played between eight salesmen. Their conversation, which is vital to the plot of the show, is delivered as rhythmic word music, intended to convey the starting, running and stopping of an old American steam train. Starting slowly, with the hiss of steam – '*Cash* for the merchandise' – the tempo increases to running speed when the clatter of wheels on rails is expressed by 'whadaya talk, whadaya talk etc'. When the train crosses points we get 'Ya can talk, talk, talk, talk, bicker, bicker, bicker etc' and when the train is climbing an incline the tempo halves to the strenuous puffing of the engine: 'Hill? Hill? Hill? Hill? etc. Eventually the train comes to rest in a cloud of steam – 'Yes sir, yes sir, yes sir . . .' All of this is unaccompanied and is a wonderful piece of onomatopoeic writing.

When tackling this I first insisted that every person involved was word perfect in the *entire* scene. Then they were encouraged to experiment with the words – to use the sibilent 's' and accentuate the aspirates; to imitate the 'doodledee, doodledah' sounds of train wheels – in other words to 'play trains' as children do. Then we concentrated on the tempo with particular emphasis on the picking up of cues – there must be no gaps in the rhythm of the train wheels. Not until these points were mastered did I start to move the characters about the stage. It entailed a lot of repetition; in the latter stages gabble rehearsals were introduced and the actors were further encouraged to do a 'warm up' before every performance. I may add that all this effort paid off!

Finally, let us turn our attention to the complicated quasi-operatic finales found in many of the older musicals. One such occurs at the end of Act 1 of *Rose-Marie*. The relevant pages are 87–9 in the vocal score published by Chappell & Co Ltd.

Study the dialogue until you know the meaning of the words. Then listen to the music and try to pick out relevant 'themes', any dramatic pauses or changes in tempo – in other words see what the music has to say. Then put words and music together. It is advisable to write the complete passage of dialogue into the score which only indicates certain cue lines.

Let us consider this section in detail. After the trio with which the finale starts, we hear the Mounties' theme (*poco marcato*). Malone and the Mounties approach, as indicated in the score, and Rose-Marie has a visual cue for her cry 'Malone!' There is ample time for Emile and Hawley to break away. At *moderato* on page 88 is the 'My Jim' motif (the love theme) and this I suggest is the appropriate cue for the dialogue which Rose-Marie introduces with 'You've always been my friend'; rather than where indicated in the score. There are ample pauses and breaks in the next seven bars to cover the dialogue until Emile speaks. His line is cued in the score. However, unless he intends to drag out this short speech, which I maintain is surely against his character, the bars marked *molto sostenuto* fit better if played *moderato* ignoring all the pauses so that the chord in the $\frac{1}{4}$ bar comes just before Rose-Marie's 'What's that you say?'

At *con molto sentimento* the 'Jim' theme reappears, and this covers the dialogue to Lady Jane's entrance.

The Indian theme, *molto moderato quasi lento* refers to the speeches concerning the death of Black Eagle and the *ad lib* timpani bar continues until Malone's 'Wanda saw him do it'.

The Mounties' theme appears again at *andante molto* and covers Malone's instructions to his men.

Rose-Marie tries once more to save her lover – 'Malone, no use to look etc' at the top of page 89, *plaintively* and this runs easily into Emile's line at *moderato*. Rose-Marie's cry from the heart, 'Please', should coincide with the pause chord in the *presto* bar and from here to the vocal line on page 90 all the dialogue must be carefully controlled so that she can speak into her singing. The music must flow quietly under the dialogue, and there are only four pauses to assist the musical director. There should be only the briefest of gaps between Rose-Marie's 'Care for him' and her 'Like ev'ry girl in all de worl' '.

Once the tempo of the dialogue in a passage such as this has been established, the actors should be instructed to maintain it at all performances in order that the musical director may know what to expect and control his orchestra accordingly. As rehearsals progress you will find that the actors will get to know instinctively whether they are in time or not and they will adjust accordingly.

[5]

Casting the show

A good cast of principals is an essential ingredient to the success of any musical and its selection is a phase of the production most subject to chance. It taxes the judgement and experience of the production team to the full and the greatest care should be taken over this operation.

In the commercial theatre a musical production is usually an independent venture where every member of the company is chosen to meet the particular needs of the show in hand. The director may call upon the services of casting agencies, use his own knowledge of the abilities of possible candidates gleaned from past productions and he may hold as many auditions as he thinks fit. Budgetary considerations, not time, are his chief consideration and he rarely has to take account of any permanent organisation. There have been cases where a production was postponed until the chosen artists were free to take up the engagement. The director of amateur musicals, on the other hand, is made only too aware of his responsibility to train and build up a permanent company as well as attending to the direction of the show. He is fighting against time and, in all but exceptional circumstances, he will be expected to cast his production from the members of an existing company. However, he should be warned of the futility of sacrificing the quality of the production for the sake of training the actors.

From their initial discussions, the director, musical director and choreographer will have started to build up a mental picture of each character in the show. They may even have made notes regarding the physical appearance, age and ability to move required by each part, and they will most certainly know what vocal qualities are required. It is even possible that they have, in their own minds, tentatively allocated the parts, if only to assure themselves that the show could be cast.

However, it is unrealistic of them to hold auditions with an absolute, photographic impression of each character. Their task is to search for certain qualities and they should attend try-outs with an open mind. In casting a show the important point is to steer a middle course between typecasting and miscasting. Beware of taking the easy way out. To choose soprano, Miss X, to play the lead, simply because she has always taken the lead and is a reliable player may gain you some temporary advantage, but your regular audience may come in time to regard Miss X as the same character in a new situation and each successive show as merely a rewrite of the last. Better far to heed C.B. Purdom's advice that 'A player should be fitted to his part — but as an actor, not as an individual.'

To have personal knowledge of parts previously undertaken by auditionees is naturally of great help in one's deliberations, if only to direct them to roles for which they are better suited, for amateurs are notorious for applying for parts for which they are unfitted. Since we are concerned with musicals, the vocal range and ability of the actors is of prime importance, and this itself will limit our choice. Equally important are the physical requirements of the role. The actor playing Franz Schubert in *Lilac Time* must not only possess the vocal range for the part, but he should also have the physical stature of the composer. It may prove necessary to give him a false stomach, but a superb soprano with an excess of avoirdupois should not, I suggest, be cast as Lilli, Mr Veit's youngest daughter in the same show! Similarly, actresses wishing to be considered for the title roles in *Annie, Anne of Green Gables* or *Annie Get Your Gun* must, in addition to possessing the acting and vocal requirements, approximate in physical build to these young persons.

The physical relationship of one part to another also needs attention. Save in exceptional circumstances, one would not cast a leading lady who is head and shoulders above the leading man.

Consideration should also be given to the possibilities of disguise by the use of makeup. Average faces can be made to appear slightly broader or slightly narrower, straight juvenile faces can be made into character faces, but makeup cannot make a character face into a juvenile face nor a very broad face seem narrow.

Apart from singing ability, some regard must be taken of the quality of the actor's speaking voice, the power, timbre, range and pace of delivery. One should seek to get voices that suit the parts and aim for a wide range of variation among the cast.

Attention should be given to the actor's ability to move. Often in a musical show, a part will call for dancing and the choreographer must be satisfied that the applicant will be able to master the steps that he or she has in mind.

A difficult quality to assess is the ability of the actor or actress to create the proper empathic effect on the audience. Some individuals who appear warm and sympathetic in real life, and even in rehearsal, freeze up in performance and appear cold and mechanical. Others, who rarely catch the eye and are dismissed as plain and frumpy, blossom under the lights and develop a stage personality and a positive allure.

Finally, a word about compatability. While experienced professionals, who may be sworn enemies in real life, may act smoothly together on stage, the same is not true of most amateurs. Should such a situation arise, you will no doubt be advised by the GMC of the society, and in this case it is probably better to sacrifice a little talent in the interests of happy teamwork.

Having said all this, it is only fair to point out that the director of amateurs is invariably short of time, candidates and money to indulge his ideas on casting and auditions are often a matter of compromise. One has to learn to 'cut one's coat according to one's cloth', since societies will often insist on presenting shows which are way above their talents and technical ability to produce; but it is this challenge of attempting the near impossible that spurs the amateur director on to greater achievements.

Do not let it be thought that auditioning is the only method used to cast amateur shows. In exceptional cases an 'ad hoc' company will be formed to present a piece where each member is invited to play a specific role or to be in the ensemble. Another example is where a choral group wishes to mount a show but is content to act in the chorus. Here again actors and actresses of proven ability will be invited to take the principal roles. However, auditions are the methods used by the majority of amateur groups and it is to the running of these that we now turn our attention.

Auditions: procedure

Soon after his appointment, the amateur director will be asked to suggest suitable passages of the libretto as audition pieces. He should select these with care, aiming to give candidates an opportunity to show as many facets of the character they wish to portray as possible. Depending on the type and size of the part, it may prove desirable to give two or even more extracts for the applicant to study. Sometimes the director will take the entire company through a reading of the libretto to give them an overall idea of the show and at the same time he can give some indication of the various characters. The musical director will likewise set certain numbers from the show which will test the auditionees' ability to cope with the range, style and various moods of the score. The choreographer may, in certain cases, set dance steps to be memorised as a test of the artiste's ability to pick up a routine and indicate his or her ability to move well, or she may simply ask applicants to prepare some point work or tap steps of their own choosing.

All the members of the company should be encouraged to attempt a role. It can be pointed out to them that the audition committee are looking more for intelligent interpretation, lively imagination and ability to think out and develop a part, than a technically polished performance. And of course the greater the selection of applicants, the easier is the task of the audition committee. Applicants should be encouraged to memorise the passages of libretto (it is very difficult to judge an actor when he has his head in a script) and to invent moves and business. I also encourage the use of properties and makeshift costume if this will assist the auditionee to make full use of his or her skills.

Auditions should be held as soon as possible after the selection of a new show since this allows the musical director ample time to rehearse the principals' music and integrate them in the ensembles before staging begins. Auditions should be held in the theatre or hall where the performances will be given, or failing this, in a hall of comparable size. Auditions may be closed, open to the members of the company to witness, or held before an invited audience. The last two choices may be said to create an atmosphere but opinions vary as to the advisability of these open auditions and, since the matter is really one of policy, it is best left to be decided by the General Management Committee.

The procedure adopted for auditions varies from one company to another and the director is advised to acquaint himself, in advance, with local custom, and arrange to alter any matter of which he strongly disapproves. Auditions may be conducted by the production team, or, as is more common, they may be joined by an 'audition committee'. A typical committee would be constituted as follows:

(1) Chairman, director, musical director, choreographer.
(2) Two persons, not connected with the society, but who have a practical working knowledge of the show under discussion.
(3) Two members of the society, elected by the company (to see fair play).
(4) A member of the General Management Committee (to advise on policy matters).

(5) The secretary of the society, *ex officio*, who takes notes and reports back to the General Management Committee.

This body sits apart and at some distance from the stage – the front of the dress circle or the middle of the stalls are good spots – the better to judge the ability of the applicants under theatre conditions.

In addition the stage manager may be in attendance to organise the auditionees plus a pianist and two or more readers-in, the latter being recruited from a neighbouring company to read the 'other' parts in the audition scenes.

Every effort should be made to put auditionees at their ease; even the most hardened, experienced player suffers from nerves on these occasions. Sometimes it is a good plan to ignore the first few moments of an audition and allow the applicant time to warm up and overcome initial nervousness. The committee should feel free to put questions on any point that may need clarification. Above all, every applicant should be treated with courtesy and given the auditioning panel's full attention; whispers or indications of boredom or impatience can easily turn the occasion into a dispiriting experience for the auditionee.

Parts should be heard in order of importance, the ideal being to select the leads and then build up a balanced cast. Whether one should discuss each group of parts in turn and arrive at a decision, or postpone discussion until all the applicants have been heard is a moot point. It is an advantage to decide as you go, but there is an inherent danger in this method in that one loses the option of considering an applicant who, although he or she has indicated no interest in one of the more important roles, nevertheless shows promise of being the ideal candidate. In most cases the type of show being auditioned will dictate the timing of discussions.

Auditions: discussions

The purpose of these discussions is to allow each member on the selection committee a chance to air his or her views. Naturally those of the director and his associates will be given most weight, but the production team should take note of the impressions and opinions of the rest of the committee. In the majority of cases the choice will be unanimous but, where opinions are sharply divided, the final selection must rest with the director, musical director and choreographer for it is they who ultimately have to produce the show.

In the main, the committee will arrive at its decisions on the basis of what they have seen, but there will be times when discussion reaches a deadlock. At this juncture it is, I believe, legitimate to introduce any other knowledge one may have of the candidate's ability. For example, it is well known that there are some actors who can give a first-class audition but who never improve on their initial reading; there are others who undergo agonies of nervous agitation at auditions but who, in rehearsal, develop a character beyond one's highest hopes. Again, one can cite the artist who, while nominally a member of the company, will play only in a principal role and, if unsuccessful, will look elsewhere for a part. Sometimes one has to sacrifice the acting for the vocal ability or vice versa. There are many precedents for this in the commercial theatre – we have already noted Rex Harrison's portrayal of Professor Higgins and the casting of Frankie Howerd as Pseudolus in *A Funny Thing Happened on the Way to the Forum* is another example. Conversely, a really good top tenor is essential for the role of Sid-el-Kar in *The Desert Song* and if the only available singer is an indifferent actor who cannot respond to intensive coaching, his part must be kept as simple as possible, even in exceptional cases, to the extent of dividing his dialogue among other characters.

When a show calls for a large number of speaking parts, it can be an advantage to allocate a number of cameo roles to one suitable candidate. The parts of the 'Selsey Man', Harry and Lord Boxington in *My Fair Lady* can easily be 'doubled', as can Mrs Hopkins and Lady Boxington. In *Bitter Sweet*, Sir Arthur Fenchurch and Herr Schlick are two parts which give an actor a chance to display contrasts in styles.

Sometimes it is essential to double. The parts of the Star Keeper and Doctor Seldon in *Carousel* are a good example since Billy Bigelow, in the final scene, remarks that Dr Seldon reminds him of 'that fellow up there on the ladder'.

Another sort of doubling occurs in *Oklahoma!* where dancers may have to double for Curley, Judd and Laurey in the 'Dream Ballet'. Naturally, they will be dressed identically but they should also approximate physically to the characters they are supposed to represent.

Children often play roles in musicals. If the part is very important, as in *Annie*, I would suggest that applicants audition in the same way as the adults. If the part is less demanding calling for mime and movement only, as in the case with the youngest Snow children in *Carousel*, the production team may prefer to try out the applicants in private, rather than subject them to the rigours of a full audition. However, in general, children attracted to stage work are surprisingly self-assured and not easily overawed.

Other considerations

Occasionally it may not prove possible to cast a part either because there are no applicants or because those that did apply did not meet the required standards. Further auditions may resolve the matter but if not one must look elsewhere for a suitable actor. In such a case, if the director is convinced that he cannot cast the part from the company, I strongly urge him to oppose any pressure to force him to allocate the part to a member of the society. He must remember that his own reputation, as well as that of the company, is affected by every production which he undertakes and it is in the interest of all parties that he keeps his standard as high as he reasonably can. Maintaining his high standard, even at the expense of inviting outsiders to play, can only benefit the society which will attract fresh talent that desires to be associated with a company of repute. The society thus builds and goes on to enjoy a wider and better choice of potential principals from among its own numbers.

If one has to go outside the company to find a suitable actor, the knowledge of other societies' work is of great assistance. When watching other amateur productions, a director should note the name of any artist whose performance impresses him. He should also endeavour to be on the closest terms with neighbouring societies since he will undoubtedly need their assistance at some time or another. NODA is another source of assistance.

Outsiders usually play by invitation but they are often asked to give an audition, as a formality, in order to satisfy all concerned that they really are of the required standard.

There is some dissension as to whether any direction should be given at auditions. Some instruction can often determine whether the applicant is able to pick up direction quickly and intelligently. It can also assist the musical director if he is allowed to test the full vocal range of a singer, or his ability to sing in concerted items with other principals.

Ideally all principal roles should be understudied. This is rarely possible. Even if there were sufficient suitable individuals to mount a double cast, neither the director nor the stage manager, who traditionally should rehearse understudies, have the time to attend to his task. Once again, with the assistance of NODA, another company that has recently presented the show or who have it in rehearsal, may be asked to stand by during the week of the production in case of mishap. Often the director and choreographer will be sufficiently talented to be able to step into a part should the actor or actress fall ill, but in any case all parts should be adequately covered.

[6]

Rehearsals: the first phase

So far in our discussions we have considered the director as an artist, and an artist he must remain until the last performance and the production is complete. But now, with the start of actual rehearsals he begins to function in another and equally important capacity – that of a teacher. Indeed the ability of every member of the production team to teach ranks almost as high as their ability as artists.

The professional director, mounting a revival of a musical for a tour – a fair comparison with an amateur company – can expect to have a fully trained company of singers, dancers and actors. Prior to dress rehearsals, intense and continuous daily rehearsals will occupy a minimum of three weeks often augmented with evening music or coaching sessions.

By contrast, the amateur company will be made up of individuals from all trades and professions. Some may have received tuition in singing or dancing, but in the main they will be untrained, united only by their love of the musical theatre. The majority will have business commitments and they will meet for three hours once or twice a week over a period of several months. Nevertheless their enthusiasm and desire to learn will often overcome these initial shortcomings and the quality of many amateur musical productions reaches a very high standard.

Rehearsals fall into four main groups: music rehearsals, under the musical director; principal rehearsals; ensemble rehearsals; and dancing rehearsals.

Music rehearsals

It is useful to devote the first music rehearsal to a complete play-through of the vocal score. Members proficient at sight-reading can sing the melodies but matters of part-singing can be ignored since the purpose of the exercise is to give the company an overall idea of the music.

Thereafter, one must accept that the first few music rehearsals will be

given up to teaching the notes by rote since, unless the ability to
sight-read is a prerequisite of entry into the company, it is safe to assume
that the majority of members cannot and have little or no knowledge of
notation. Naturally one cannot give a crash course on music but it may
prove a valuable exercise when starting a new show to explain the basic
symbols used in notation – even at the risk of boring the more know-
ledgeable members for a while. Obviously one will avoid using technical terms wherever possible.

An important ally for the musical director is a really first-rate rehearsal
accompanist – or several if the budget will allow. One should not
attempt to teach too much in a rehearsal session, for it is essential that all
members absorb their parts. They should be encouraged to make notes
of any instructions given in their scores in their own words – where the
technical terms are crescendo or pianissimo they may prefer to write
'gradually get louder' or 'very soft'. Many great conductors have made
recordings of their rehearsal sessions, and a musical director can learn
much by listening to these. A good illustration, albeit applied to an
orchestra, occurs on the disc of Bruno Walter working, with the
Columbia Symphony Orchestra, on the first movement of Mozart's
'Linz' symphony K425 (*Phillips, ABL 3161 – The Birth of a Performance*).
The strings and woodwinds are finding difficulty with their note values
in the opening bars. The maestro does not discuss quavers, semi-quavers
or rests. Instead he cries 'Too long! You should be able to say "off" to
yourself' (between each phrase). This type of tuition, apart from being
fun, is easily absorbed by untrained singers. It is good for the morale of
the chorus to conclude each session with a sing-through of the items
which have been rehearsed.

The musical director has to work to a deadline – that being when the
director wants to start staging. It is better, therefore, to complete the
score as quickly as possible, learning the correct notes and adding the
dynamics once this has been done. When words and music have been
memorised, the ensemble should intermingle and move about whilst
singing, thus gaining confidence in holding their own line against
others, as they will later have to do in staging rehearsals.

Diction and enunciation will call for a lot of attention. The initial
renderings of the title song from *White Horse Inn* will invariably come
out as 'Wye Tor Sin', and, in the same show, is a duet which can sound
as 'Yaw Rise' (Your Eyes). Singers should be instructed to sing on the
vowel sound; to avoid the lingering 's' at the end of words – the trick is
to open the mouth as soon as the 's' is sounded; to use the ee-oo dipthong

in words such as 'you' (avoid the nasal 'yew' like the plague); to use the labial 'l' in words such as 'love' and to stress the first beat in the bar. However, avoid being too pedantic and suit the diction to the style of the show. Diction in *No, No Nanette* is vastly different from that required of the cockneys in *Jorrocks* or the more relaxed delivery of *Godspell*. Cultivate the use of lips, teeth and tongue and, above all, avoid the type of singing of the 'foot in the pub door' approach.

The MD is sometimes asked to teach the music for the principal's vocal auditions. I can see no harm in his doing so, provided that equal opportunities are offered to all aspiring leads, so that no accusations of favouritism can be levelled later. Ideally, though, each candidate should prepare their audition pieces without the assistance of any member of the auditioning panel.

Once a show has been cast there must be rehearsals for the principals. These are better held on other than chorus nights and may be held in private houses. It is important that the musical director runs through the whole of each singer's music and gives a clear indication of what is required. Phrasing should be marked so that each number can be practised privately in accordance with the MD's markings. Once they are familiar with their music, the principals can be incorporated into the ensemble rehearsals.

It is up to the MD to decide when the company should lay aside their scores but it is essential that all music is more or less committed to memory by the time the show goes 'on the floor'.

However well the music has been prepared prior to staging, the musical director must accept that many of the finer points will suffer during floor rehearsals, as the company struggle with lines and movement. This can be remedied by holding one or two music-only rehearsals during the later period of rehearsals in order to polish up the vocal side of the production.

Occasionally a singer is asked to perform in circumstances which are hardly inducive to good vocal production. In *Véronique*, the unfortunate leading lady has two duets in Act 2, one delivered from the back of a donkey, the other whilst being pushed in a swing. In such circumstances, the director and musical director must seek a compromise which will give the singer every chance to make a good impression.

During rehearsals questions will arise concerning details of tempo, interpretation and the actual staging. These should be fully discussed by the production team as they occur, and any changes implemented only when they serve to improve the show as a whole.

Principal's rehearsals

Once the show has been cast, and while the chorus are learning the score, the director will be rehearsing the principals. Initially actors tend to see the show from their own viewpoint and although the director must give them every opportunity of using their talents to the full, he must keep an overall view and relate the various parts to a homogeneous whole.

The prompt-book will be the foundation of all the director's work. How he communicates his ideas to his cast will depend on his personality and the experience and personalities of his cast and the amount of rehearsal time available. Experienced actors often need the merest suggestion from the director to enable them to develop a role. Some will be stimulated to the right approach through questions, analogies and improvisation. Others may require demonstrations, both physically and vocally of what is required. But many amateurs appear to need a more autocratic approach, where every move, gesture and nuance of speech is dictated by the director. Whatever course is chosen, the director must remember that, ultimately, the character belongs to the actor. Above all be prepared to amend any piece of business or movement that an actor finds ·difficult to portray.

The first practical step is to have a read-through with the cast. Some directors – W.S. Gilbert was one – like to read the play themselves, playing all the roles. Others allow the actors to read their own parts. The latter course is not always successful, since actors are not always good readers. However, their main desire at this stage is to say their lines aloud, and for no other reason, this is the course I always adopt.

Preface the reading with a few words about the show and give a brief outline of the characters involved. Then take the cast through the entire play, omitting the musical items, but giving all the cuts and alterations. Resist the temptation to correct any faults at this juncture, making notes of them for correction at a future date.

Some directors, who follow Stanislavsky's method of acting technique, devote much time at this stage to discussions of characterisation and motivation. Sir Laurence Olivier is reputed to have shown his impatience of this school of thought in an interview in *The New York Times* '. . . an actor gets the thing right by doing it over and over. Arguing about motivation and so forth is a lot of rot.'

Blocking

If the director has prepared his prompt-book along the lines already discussed, he will find his task considerably eased. Neither the musical director, nor the accompanist is required at this stage, although they may give musical coaching to principals not required for any scene.

Make certain that the cast underline their parts in their scripts. This is a valuable aid to finding one's place and the act of marking up a book is, in itself, an aid to learning the part. In addition ensure that everyone is familiar with the designations of the various areas of the stage (see Fig. 5) and appreciates that directions are given from the actor's viewpoint.

Start the rehearsal with a detailed description of the setting. Models or blackboard diagrams can assist in this respect. One method is to mark out the set, full size, on the rehearsal floor. Tape, chalk lines or chairs can be used to indicate the boundaries of the setting, the entrances and any furniture.

The director goes through the show line by line, giving the moves and business and these details are noted by the cast in their scripts. No hand properties are used at these blocking rehearsals, the prime purpose being to give each actor some work to study. The last hour of these rehearsals is spent playing through the blocked scenes, without interruption, as revision for the actors and to satisfy the director that his instructions have been understood. These rehearsals should be augmented with private practice, either singly or in groups and blocking sets the foundation for this essential homework.

How soon should the words be committed to memory, for, until they have learned their parts, the actors cannot proceed to the next stage of rehearsals? Professional actors are often required to learn a part in a week, and whilst the manner in which they do this may be a purely mechanical process, professionals usually have enough technical knowledge of their art to be able to differentiate between the *words* and the *meaning*. On the other hand, if an amateur starts memorising his part before the director has discussed and blocked the scenes, he may well come up with an interpretation which is contrary to what the director has envisaged and, worse, he will probably find great difficulty in unlearning his mistakes! For this reason I insist that no lines are learned until the part has been blocked and I am satisfied that the actor understands the meaning of his lines and the moves involved. Once these points have been established the words should be memorised as quickly as possible.

There are various aids to help get rid of the book. The very act of reading the lines whilst walking through the moves and business is one; others include writing out the pages of dialogue in full (all the speeches, not just the actor's part); using a tape-recorder or reading the script prior to sleep. The individual must find the method which best suits him. I would recommend that the director gives notice of the deadline, after which no scripts will be allowed at rehearsals.

Many shows call for specialised business – the sword fights in *The Three Musketeers* and the circus acts in *Barnum* are examples – and, if the director has not the practical knowledge to undertake this side of the production, the work should be undertaken by a specialist. The teaching and coaching of any dance routines is the premise of the choreographer. Extra rehearsal time must be allocated for this special training which should be initiated once the cast is selected.

Experiment

After the blocking rehearsals have been completed, the director will rehearse the principals in self-contained segments – these may be complete scenes or 'french' scenes – gradually building up each act. I prefer to direct on stage or, if in a rehearsal room, close to the cast since, at this juncture, one is constantly halting the action to adjust or correct. Later, when the show is more advanced, I will view the rehearsals from a distance.

Initially one concentrates on the moves and the meanings of the lines, seeking confirmation that one's preliminary plotting and interpretation are both logical and practical. At the same time the actors are groping their way to a basic understanding of their parts. Discussion is encouraged, but only about the individual's own part, never about another actor's interpretation. Properties are now introduced. In shows such as *Fiddler on the Roof* instruction may be necessary on special rites or habits; agreement is reached on the pronunciation of unusual names or places and, in period productions, details of manners and style are considered. At this point continuity is unimportant. It is a good plan to work on the most difficult scenes and to pay special attention to the beginning and ending of each act.

Much of the time will be spent dealing with the meaning of the text. Should an actor find difficulty with a line, ask him to explain it in his own words. A simple phrase, such as 'What do you want?' can be delivered in a number of ways depending upon which word is stressed:

'*What* do you want?' (Tell me what it is that you require.)

'What *do* you want?' (Having suggested several alternatives, I still don't know.)

'What do *you* want?' (Oh, it's you. Well, what is it?)

'What do you *want*?' (I know you need something, but what is it?)

Insist that the actors listen to the lines spoken to them, since the clue to the mood and the correct response is often contained in them. Save in very exceptional circumstances, the director should avoid giving the correct reading for the actor to imitate, the purpose being to get the players to find it through experimentation and mental effort. These initial sessions are a time for experiment and everyone, from director to the smallest bit-players, should reassess and refine their ideas in the light of these rehearsals.

Staging the principal's musical numbers

To utilise the talents and time of the musical director and pianist to the full, it is advisable to set aside special rehearsals for the principal's musical numbers, delaying these until the libretto has been blocked so that the actors involved will have some idea of the context of the number and the emotional approach to be adopted. This is important in the modern musical where the song carries forward the action, rather than being merely an interpolation as is often the case in the older type of show.

Initially one should study the lyrics as a piece of spoken dialogue, seeking to understand the meaning of the words, and the emotions and business they suggest. Then, listen to the music; see what it has to say, the mood it expresses. Pay particular attention to the orchestral passages where the voice is tacit, considering these on similar lines to those already discussed in the section on 'Dialogue over music'.

Perhaps the most difficult to set is a solo delivered alone on the stage with no one to play to. Soliloquies in the Shakespearian mode, these are numbers such as 'If I were a rich man' from *Fiddler on the Roof* or the 'Soliloquy' in *Carousel* and they require careful and detailed analysis in the staging. Sometimes it is possible to use a property as a focal-point; an example would be the photograph to which Bill Hickock sings 'Higher than a Hawk' in *Calamity Jane*.

With duets, trios and quartets, arrange the non-singer or singers down stage of, and facing, the soloist to provide a focal-point, until they regroup to join the vocal line; try a practice study with the 'Jolly Brothers' quartet from *Lilac Time*.

Sometimes a static picture is the answer; this often occurs in the Savoy Operas — 'Strange Adventure' from *The Yeomen of the Guard*, and 'Brightly Dawns our Wedding Day' from *The Mikado* being examples where this ploy succeeds.

Mark the moves, business and expression over the relevant bars in the score. These will be the basic blueprint which can be adapted as work proceeds for the soloists will often contribute valuable ideas of their own. Position soloists well downstage. This aids projection and the MD will have better control over them but remember that there are many other positions than DC. Keep moves to a minimum, and wherever possible let these be made during the orchestral passages rather than when the artist is singing. When a gesture is called for let it be big — made from the shoulder — and always try to use all the music. Bear in mind that a singer needs an unrestricted diaphragm — something which I feel the composer of *Robert and Elizabeth* overlooked when he gave Elizabeth some rather difficult top notes whilst reclining on a day bed.

By the time the ensemble take to the floor, the principals should have a sound idea of their words, moves and business, leaving the director free to concentrate fully on the chorus.

Chorus rehearsals

Directors are urged to be patient and even-tempered at all times, particularly when dealing with amateurs. I must confess however that, when dealing with the ensemble, I find this a very difficult dictum to follow, especially with those members who are unpunctual and irregular attenders and who treat rehearsals as a social occasion rather than a working session. The professional director can voice his disapproval in no uncertain terms but his amateur counterpart is expected to restrain his feelings. Therefore make matters quite clear at the first staging rehearsal concerning punctuality and regular attendance; explain that the show is a team effort depending for its success on the co-operation of every single member and that there are no small parts, only small actors. Having said which it is obvious that the director will have to ensure that he attends rehearsals punctually, with his plan of campaign clearly worked out in advance — another reason for the careful preparation of the prompt book. Start on time — even if only half a dozen members are present; once the company realise that you mean business they will arrive regularly and on time.

The chorus may find difficulty in retaining their moves and business from one rehearsal to another. Encourage them to write their directions over the appropriate bars in their scores immediately after a rehearsal and then revise the work before attending the next session.

Aim to keep the majority of the chorus fully employed. Many vocal numbers are for men's or women's voices only; when staging these items, arrange for the men to attend at the usual time with the ladies joining for full ensembles an hour later. Taking this arrangement turn and turn about will be generally appreciated by the busy housewife or businessman.

Seek the co-operation of the management committee to keep any chatter, refreshment breaks (beloved of amateurs), company notices and announcements to a minimum so that all the available rehearsal time is used to the best advantage.

If new to a company, the director may experience difficulty in identifying the various members of his ensemble. A useful tip is to issue each member with a coloured tag, named and numbered in accordance with the plots in the prompt-book. Referring back to the *White Horse Inn* ensemble (see Figs. 12–17) the maids (sopranos) could have red tags lettered A–I; the guides (tenors) a yellow tag numbered I–VI; flower girls (contraltos) green tags lettered a–f and so on.

Chorus work falls into a variety of styles. At the simplest there are the Gilbert and Sullivan operas – equal numbers of men and women who dress the stage, usually in symmetrical patterns. Good choral tone and the minimum of business is generally the order of the day. Shows such as *Show Boat* or *Finian's Rainbow* call for a double chorus, one white, the other coloured, with opportunities for cameo acting parts.

In *Anne of Green Gables, Oliver!* and *The Music Man* the chorus are divided into adults, teenagers and children. That in *A Little Night Music* is very small and acts almost like a 'classic' chorus, commenting on the action, sometimes part of it, sometimes apart from it.

In recent years the marked division between the principal players, chorus and dancers has been gradually eroded and there is an increasing emphasis on a choral group playing multiple roles as is evidenced in shows such as *Hair, Pippin* and *Godspell.*

When setting the chorus members' positions on stage, the ability of each one to see the conductor's baton is a prime consideration. Sometimes it is advisable to keep the vocal parts together, especially with a complex score requiring divided parts and I would also recommend doing so when dealing with a young, inexperienced company.

A good general rule is to place the taller members in the back and outside positions so as not to block the view of the shorter ones, though such advice need not be adhered to too rigidly. One should aim for a series of aesthetically pleasing compositions which are psychologically in keeping with the mood of the scene. Symmetrical groupings are not always necessary, nor are they always desirable. Many factors dictate the areas of the stage to be peopled by the chorus – the shape of the setting, the lighting design, the number and variety of the entrances and the different playing levels to name a few. If the production is played on a thrust stage or 'in the round' the disposition of the chorus is even more critical.

A basic principle to employ when positioning the ensemble is to built the composition in small triangular groups. Vary the heights: have some people sitting or kneeling; use steps or rostra. When all the chorus are positioned, view the composition from all angles, and from above, and adjust as necessary. For inspiration, study the paintings of the masters, noting the composition, the lighting and the positions of hands and feet; in particular examine the handling of crowd scenes in films and on television.

When setting a chorus entry, place the cast in the picture required and then explain how they enter and move to these positions – in other words, work backwards! Occasionally the chorus are required to enter *en masse*, but wherever possible cue the entrances of individual groups, spreading the cues over the introductory music or dialogue, so that the ensemble enter gradually and are assembled by the time they are required to sing.

If the chorus has to enter singing, try to arrange that some of the stronger, reliable vocalists arrive on stage a little in advance, so that they can see the conductor and act as leaders.

Pay equal attention to the exeunt of the chorus. Spread the departure, giving cue phrases for different sections to leave, so that the crowd appears to melt away. Check any tendency to 'bunch up' at exits; insist that each player continues acting and moving until well clear of the stage. This is particularly important with a marching exit. Many of the older shows include 'military' numbers – those in *The Desert Song* and *The New Moon* being very well known. Planned like a drill sequence, actions are timed to occur on the strong beat in the bar on specific cue words, and the routine is practised repeatedly until absolute precision is achieved. These numbers may be taken at a slower speed until the routine has been mastered and then brought up to the proper tempo. Nearly every musical contains concerted items which will benefit from a well-drilled routine as 'The Entry of the Peers' in *Iolanthe*, the *Oklahoma!* chorus, 'Stop the clocks' in *The Ambassador* and 'One' in *A Chorus Line* illustrate.

This is not to say that every number should consist of a series of stereotyped moves and hackneyed gestures performed in unison. The tendency in modern productions is to treat the ensemble as a collection of individuals, each with his or her own specific character. The chorus continues to work as a corporate body, but individuals react to the action of the play within the confines of their particular character. After explaining to the company the context and purpose of the scene under rehearsal, and describing the action, the actors are positioned as already described. Some individual instruction is now necessary: explain clearly to each group what types of characters they portray, how they are involved in the action and what their probable reactions will be. Cue words are allocated for entrances and important moves, but the actors are encouraged to develop their parts for themselves. Let them overplay their parts initially – it is easy to adjust the acting once the sequence is established. This method gives the director an idea of the capabilities of each chorus member and he will be able to earmark the most promising for more important roles.

Rabbles, market scenes, the natural-seeming comings and goings in a busy street scene, all these have to be meticulously thought out when preparing the prompt-book. Actual paths of movement have to be defined, properties and business researched for authenticity. There should be a rhythm to the ebb and flow of the whole action, yet, should the eye linger on one spot, there should still be discernible the individual characters who make up the homogeneous whole.

Possibly the chorus work requiring most mental concentration occurs in scenes where they have no music or dialogue to perform, but are used to dress and give atmosphere as occurs in large parts of the ballroom scenes in *Pink Champagne* or *My Fair Lady*. They will be required to mime, but initially it is useful to invent some dialogue and action to help to get the business established in their minds before reverting to mime only. The director must indicate what parts of the principal's dialogue should be ignored by the ensemble and which are heard and reacted to.

A warming-up or limbering-up session before rehearsals start is time well spent. This can be under the control of the choreographer. Having been engaged with business matters or housework for most of the day most of the cast will need stimulating, both physically and mentally, before embarking on a rehearsal. Everyone, from the leading players to the newest chorus member, should be encouraged to join in the simple exercises, performed to musical accompaniment. If time allows, some simple improvisation, based on situations likely to arise in the show, will prove valuable. Finally, before getting down to rehearsal proper, a sing-through of a really rousing chorus number will serve to clear the tubes and open up the lungs!

Dancing rehearsals

Many directors are also accomplished choreographers and undertake the setting and rehearsal of all the dance routines. While a practical knowledge of stage dancing is an advantage, it is by no means an essential part of the director's make-up; what is required is a sympathetic understanding of the choreographer's task and the ability to express ideas for the choreographer to translate into dances.

In most of the shows written before 1945 – the pre-*Oklahoma!* days – the dancers in a show were just that – a troupe who entered for a musical item, danced and left. In today's shows dancers will be part of the ensemble, they may play small parts and their routines will evolve naturally from the story and the situation. Thus it is advisable to schedule dancing rehearsals for nights other than those set for full company rehearsals when the troupe will be required by the director.

The demands made on the dancers will vary from show to show and many require a variety of styles and techniques – a point to bear in mind when choosing a show. For this reason it is recommended that dancers are auditioned for each show. The director and musical director may assist in this difficult task, but the final choice must be left to the choreographer. Dancers are usually the younger members of the company and, apart from their technical ability, one should consider their heights since the ideal is to have a 'matching set'. This is easier said than done and one will usually have to take the best of the talent available. Of recent years it has become easier to find men willing to join the ranks of the dancers but trained male soloists are rare. They are usually training for the professional stage, tend to be in great demand and share their talent among several companies.

Normally the troupe will be built on a core of a few good, trained dancers and it is around these that the routines will be planned. The untrained ones can be given very simple steps and movements and used to dress the stage. If necessary, cut the total number used in certain routines – better a team of six, good, slick dancers than a dozen or more who are only second best.

Dancers need space. The director should bear this in mind when preparing his prompt-book but it is often necessary to clear or rearrange furniture to accommodate a dance. With a little ingenuity, this can be incorporated into the stage business. Sometimes it may be advisable to clear the chorus from the stage, leaving only a token number to dress the scene while a dance proceeds. Such matters should be noted and discussed at the early planning conferences.

The dancing instructor should make a point of seeing the proposed dancing costumes; they should be full enough to allow free movement; skirt lengths of any set should be uniform; if national costumes requiring boots, are called for, ensure that footwear will be supplied. Check the colour schemes, accessories, head-dresses and other details.

It is a wise precaution to check that the dance music published in the printed vocal scores is identical to that contained in the band parts. I have known an occasion where the piano score was several bars shorter than the orchestral score which caused consternation and much waste of time at band-call.

Agree all repeats, cuts and other alterations with the musical director and ensure that the rehearsal pianist's score is correctly marked up with these revisions. Check also that the accompanist is conversant with the agreed tempo of the routines. When arranging the dance plots it can be a help for the choreographer to have the music recorded on tape or cassette.

Dancing rehearsals should start soon after the show has been chosen and the dancers selected. Early rehearsals can be used to teach various steps rather than embarking on a routine. It is one way to sort out the sheep from the goats, and it gives the trained dancers a basis to work from. Since some of the troupe will be trying to do stage dancing for the first time, technical terms should be avoided. Use words which they can understand: 'jump', 'bend', 'turn' and so on, and use practical demonstration as much as possible. Routines need not be rehearsed in sequence; indeed it is often better to work on small sections at a time, and build the routine rather as one would complete a jigsaw puzzle.

Above all, rehearse to perfection. A slick, well-rehearsed routine, however simple, will be appreciated by the majority of your audience, few of whom will know much about actual dancing technique.

[7]

Rehearsals: the second phase

We move on eight to ten weeks in our production schedule. Some sixteen rehearsal sessions will have taken place and the basic blocking of principals and chorus should now be completed and the dancing routines roughed out. Now it is time to assess the progress of the production.

The first run-through

Provision will have been made in the rehearsal schedule for a number of full-day rehearsals. Sundays are usually convenient days for these. Speaking from experience, I find devoting a morning call to the principals, followed by a full company call in the afternoon, achieves the best results.

Do not expect too much from the initial run-through. Its purpose is to give everyone involved – production team, technical staff and the company – a chance to appraise the overall state of the show.

For the director it is primarily to reassure him that the cast has understood his directions and *that nothing wrong is being learned*. It also allows him to see how the principals are developing their roles and whether they are beginning to play as a team; he can reappraise the chorus groupings, the ensemble interplay and check the stage pictures, always bearing in mind the limitations of space, settings and the lighting which he has in mind. Finally, he can see whether the cast are interpreting the musical with the correct emphasis.

The musical director will be able to judge the state of the singing; to see how much of his initial teaching needs revising, check the timing of cues for musical items and note if, and where, the principals or chorus will need cueing for difficult musical entrances.

The choreographer's problems will revolve around details of entrances and exits, space, tempi and stage pictures. It will probably be the first time that she has seen her dances incorporated into the production.

For the cast, and the ensemble in particular, this is the rehearsal where the unrelated chorus blockings fall into place, and they become aware of the importance of their contribution to the show.

Often this is the first rehearsal which the full stage crew attend. Until now they will have been preparing the technical details of the production from scripts and cue sheets and will have little idea what the show looks or sounds like. At this rehearsal they arrange the settings, the positions of the furniture and properties and check the lighting, effects and curtain cues, the time available for scene changes and other backstage details involved in the running of a show.

There may be passages which, for one reason or another, have not been set, but one should attempt to do a complete run-through, even if, at times, words or music are spoken or sung without any stage action. This helps the continuity and gives an initial running time, apart from highlighting the sections which need the director's attention. Some idea of the timing of the show is important at this stage, for it affects both the cast (who may have quick costume changes to time) and the technical crew who have rapid scene changes to deal with. All incidental music should be included together with the overture and any entr'actes.

Ideally this rehearsal should be on the stage where the show will be presented. If this is impractical, a hall should be used, large enough for the stage area to be marked out to scale, and with room for the director and choreographer to view the proceedings from a distance. This is the time to get away from the stage and look at the production from all angles, including from above if the theatre has balconies and circles. Judge whether the stage pictures and dance patterns are acceptable from all parts of the house and that there is no unnecessary masking. Minor errors can be corrected as the rehearsal progresses during which the director, musical director, choreographer and stage manager will be taking copious notes. These they give to the company at the end of the rehearsal, pointing out the weak spots and the parts which require special attention, as well as giving praise where it is due. Questions from the company should be resolved where possible, or noted for attention at an early rehearsal. Above all try to end the rehearsal, which will have been a long and taxing one for most of the company, on an optimistic note. The day ends with a production meeting to assess progress and plan the second phase of rehearsals.

The polishing stage

Two or three rehearsals will be taken up with matters arising from the run-through, after which one can embark on this all-important stage of production and one that is, for me, the most satisfying. Few amateur companies allow sufficient time for polishing a show and I believe that the fault lies with the director who allows blocking rehearsals and the learning of lines and moves to draw out indefinitely. One way to overcome the difficulty is to announce certain rehearsals as polishing rehearsals, and to carry them out as such. A professional company will have several 'try-outs' before an audience prior to their opening night. Amateurs rarely play more than a week and therefore cannot use this method to achieve a polish on their performances.

Polishing a show involves questions of meaning, cadence or inflection, vocal quality, response and enunciation as well as ironing out the difficulties inherent in playing love scenes, eating on stage and similar situations.

Understanding the lines

Although the principals will have a good grasp of their lines there may still be some lack of understanding of them. This should now be remedied. A method frequently applied, and one I use myself, is to question the actor on any points of interpretation of which he appears doubtful. 'Is this line important for the audience?' 'Has it a double meaning?' 'Does it refer back to something already discussed?' 'Is it a laugh line?' 'To whom is it particularly directed?' 'Does it require an answer?' It may prove necessary to get the actor to put a speech into his own words to see whether he has really grasped the meaning. Lines are often misunderstood because many actors do not listen to what is being said by others on the stage. They should, at all times, be encouraged to listen to the dialogue as though they had never heard it before. Not only will they gain a better understanding of the script but they will also develop a method of reacting which William Gillette has termed 'the illusion of the first time'.

Pace and cue bite

Lack of pace in the delivery of dialogue is a far too common fault in amateur productions. It usually stems from the actors being uncertain of their lines. A speech, delivered by A, concludes with a cue for B; there is a pause — small but perceptible; then B wakes up and replies. Add together such pauses throughout the show and between five to ten minutes' extra playing time can result. In real-life conversations we tend to anticipate and make our responses quickly; indeed we often interrupt, and when pauses do occur they are usually the result of uncertainty, or made for special emphasis. Gabble rehearsals, in which the actors literally gabble their speeches with no thought for meaning or inflection, will help to speed the dialogue. Another way to achieve cue bite is to start one's lines as the other actor begins to say the last word of his; take care, however, that the dialogue does not degenerate into an unintelligible babble.

Individual pace

The overall pace of the scene should not be confused with the individual pace of each character. Too often one hears an actor delivering his lines at exactly the same speed as the one who was addressing him. Every character has a speed of speaking which is inherent in the part being portrayed. The young von Trapp children will speak faster than their rather taciturn Papa; Henry Higgins has a quicker delivery than Colonel Pickering or his mother. Moreover, a character will vary the speed of speaking depending upon who is being addressed. Anna, in *The King and I*, will use a faster delivery to her son than when she is speaking to the King or the King's children.

Style

In every show there should be an overall, homogeneous style of playing — a point which was once brought home to me by a Drama Adjudicator. If one is presenting *The Vagabond King* in a broad swashbuckling style all the parts should be played in this convention; similarly, if attempting a naturalistic production of *Charlie Girl*, everyone should develop their parts in this style.

Broken lines

Musical libretti abound with incomplete sentences — the ones that end . . . These can spell trouble for the amateur actor who delivers the line exactly as written, stopping at the dashes, and hoping that the other artist will come in promptly. It never works! The technique is to continue with a made-up ending and let oneself be interrupted.

Inflections are easier to explain since one can draw illustrations from music itself. A sentence is likened to a tune, starting on either an upward or a downward scale, delivered in a series of long smooth legato phrases or in short staccato snatches. Terms such as crescendo or diminuendo can also be used to a musical company.

Long speeches

These often need to be broken up with suitable business or variations of tempo or facial expression. Above all the imagination of the actor must be brought into play and constantly stimulated by the director; questioning him about his thoughts or reactions in the given situation will help.

Entrances and exits

These can be another cause of delays, and the trouble lies with actors and actresses who take their script literally. The author writes dialogue for A and B. At the end of one of B's speeches he writes 'Enter C'. In the wings C waits, ready for the end of B's line, then steps on stage. He will have four or five metres to travel before speaking so there is a delay of several seconds. The director must decide at what point in A and B's dialogue he requires C to be at a given spot on the stage and must give C an earlier cue to enable him to accomplish this. Thus, as B ends his speech, C is in position and beginning to speak.

With exits one should arrange for the character leaving the stage, to move to, or be close to, the exit so that having delivered the parting line, he may leave as speedily as possible, and the action be allowed to continue.

Laugh lines

In general, if the humour lies in the line, the line should be spoken out to the audience. The actor should not drop his voice at the end of the speech, nor turn away too quickly, but rather follow through as a golfer. Time must be allowed for the audience to react – if the action continues too quickly they will be undecided whether or not they are supposed to laugh. However, with a succession of laugh lines, it may be advisable to pick up cues quicker on the earlier ones in order to get the big laugh at the end. Do not attempt to play through laughter; hold everything (in character) until the peak has been reached and the laughter begins to subside.

Above all, beware of anticipating laughter; lines which have caused a laugh at rehearsal may get no response in performance, whereas others may bring gusts of unexpected mirth.

The rhythm of the show

Most shows proceed by a series of small climaxes to a major one which concludes the first half. The second half continues to build in a similar fashion until the main climax of the show is reached, the plot resolved and the tensions fall away slightly for the final curtain. The cast should be made aware of this rhythm and encouraged to pace their performances accordingly.

Love scenes

Love scenes need careful rehearsal until the actors are thoroughly sure of their words and movements. Guard against rigid poses. Encourage the players to act boldly; check any fumbling in the embraces — this will invariably cause a laugh — and, above all, act sincerely. A love duet sung in stereotyped poses, the lovers facing each other, clumsily grasping each other's hands, not only looks bad but it does nothing for the projection of the vocal line. It is far more satisfactory for the girl to stand in front and a little to one side of the man, so that her head appears to rest on his shoulder; his arms lightly grasp her, taking care not to restrict her breathing. Both can then sing out to the audience, and not, as so often happens, into each other's faces and the wings.

Kissing, on stage, can be the cause of embarrassment to inexperienced players. Once again, detailed analysis and rehearsal are called for. Bear in mind that many varieties of kiss exist — the gentle peck, the brush on the cheek, the nibble at the ear. The lip-to-lip kiss is rarely called for. Try to suit the type of kiss to the situation and mood of the scene and avoid any ungainly postures.

Pronunciation and dialect

Any marked peculiarity of pronunciation should be suppressed unless it is of use to the character being portrayed, and any laziness in pronunciation should be checked. When unfamiliar names of people or places occur, the director should seek advice on the accepted pronunciation of these and ensure that all the cast use the agreed pronunciation.

Musicals have been set in a variety of countries: the United States, France, Ireland, Austria, Japan and so on; the question arises whether one should play the show in the dialect of the country concerned, and here I would say emphatically 'No'. Certain characters may give a suggestion of the appropriate dialect to their lines — very often it assists in the characterisation, but to allow all and sundry to speak in a stage Scots in *Brigadoon* or with a Peruvian accent in *Nina Rosa* is to court disaster. Better to find the salient features of the language and to incorporate these, carefully and with restraint, avoiding any unnecessary exaggeration.

Polishing the music

The standard of singing and vocal interpretation will fall during the staging rehearsals, but once the cast have assimilated their moves and business, attention can be re-directed to the musical side of the production. Check that the inner vocal parts are being retained, especially the second soprano, contralto and baritone lines. Look for a good attack and pay attention to correct note values, particularly the final chords of an ensemble, to ensure that the singers come off the chord together. Whilst they are singing, encourage the cast to listen to those about them in order to appreciate a sense of vocal balance, and to think about the words that they are singing. Questioning techniques, similar to those applied to the principals, can help. Diction will also require attention and any slovenliness eradicated. Particular points to watch for are the final consonants — 'd', 't' and 'n' — and the lingering 's'.

A perennial cry from MDs is to 'watch the stick', yet the director must check any tendency by the chorus to stare at the conductor. A demonstration will show them that it is possible to see cues from out of the corner of the eye without any necessity to stare fixedly at the conductor. Cues should, in any case, be anticipated, the chorister positioning himself in such a way as to be able to see the stick easily.

Entrances and exits: the ensemble

Apart from the vocal side, the chorus will need polish in a number of departments. In the 'loose, individual chorus work', check that all entrances are begun from well off stage. There is nothing worse than to see members of the ensemble 'popping' on stage, often looking back to wave on others. Time spent in coaching individual groups, giving them definite business to develop will pay dividends. Guard against members of the chorus walking in time to the music. They should move in the manner and at the speed of the character they are meant to portray. Watch for fussy hand movements and the temptation to touch one another – we use our hands very sparingly in real life. When a gesture is required let it be big and made from the shoulder. When mime is called for, or ad lib conversational chatter, get the members to make up their own suitable lines and develop these into mime or chatter. Concentrate the attention to the focal point and encourage all to listen to the dialogue as though they were hearing it for the first time – this will result in excellent reaction and by-play, on cue!

Keep a constant eye on the groupings and stage pictures and continually view these from all parts of the theatre or hall. Regimented routines – marching songs, and the like – must be rehearsed at every session to reach absolute precision. Hand properties are now used at all rehearsals; apart from getting the cast used to handling them, one will be able to note any problems regarding their placing and disposal.

It is not unusual to find within the company enthusiastic members of rather mature years who find complicated routines a little beyond their ability to perform well. To compensate from dropping them from a difficult number it is often possible to give them small 'walk-on' parts, but do make certain that they are thoroughly rehearsed in their duties. This leads me to a cautionary tale: an old stager was given the part of a waiter in *Annie Get Your Gun*. He had to cross the set, well downstage and, as he passed Annie, take her plate of salad and place it on his tray, without breaking step. He performed perfectly at rehearsals but, on the opening night, as he snatched the plate away, the salad flew off and over the MD and pit orchestra! The conductor was festooned with lettuce and tomato and, for the next couple of nights, several of the strings were playing wrong notes since some tomato pips has adhered to their band parts.

Continuity

After these refresher courses, the show is put together again and played for continuity, the aim being to achieve an overall balance and ensure that the show moves smoothly to the final climax. Interruptions should now be avoided. Devote a session to each act in turn, giving notes at the end of the act, and then, if time permits, play the act again. If limbering-up is not a regular feature of rehearsals it should be introduced at this stage prior to starting the act.

To sum up briefly on the polishing stage:

(1) Test your stage pictures from all angles, bearing in mind the sight-lines.

(2) Watch rehearsals from far back and from all parts of the auditorium, checking for audibility and visibility.

(3) Watch for any stiff or unnatural moves. Find out why they appear so, and amend accordingly. Seek to simplify whenever possible.

(4) Make certain that the significant lines – the plot – come across.

(5) Make certain that each act opens and closes with a bang!

(6) Be certain that the actors fully understand the meaning of their lines.

(7) Watch the speed of the dialogue and check any tendency to drag.

(8) See that the actors do not pick up each other's speed of delivery.

(9) Watch for any long speeches that require breaking down.

(10) Study the playing of love scenes.

(11) Suppress any tendency to overplay an accent or dialect.

(12) Teach the actors how to play laughs and take applause.

(13) Watch the chorus reactions and ensure that they support the central theme.

(14) Encourage the effect of 'for the first time'.

[8]

Rehearsals: the final phase and dress rehearsals

Bar the usual troubles that so often bedevil even the best-organised amateur companies — sickness, change of cast, and members leaving — the show should be consolidating about two weeks before the opening night, and this is the target to aim for. A second weekend rehearsal is called and, as before, everyone concerned with the production attends, but this time the stage manager and his crew run the rehearsal as they would a performance. Properties are now used as a matter of course and any special ones such as firearms, swords or similar accoutrements should be hired for these last rehearsals so that the cast can become accustomed to using them.

The consumption of food is often an integral part of stage business — the dinner consumed in *Hello Dolly!* is an example — and suitable comestibles should be provided and the business rehearsed. Other specialised properties now brought into use would include the firecracker that Tommy uses in *The Music Man*, the ice-creams used in *Anne of Green Gables* and the bottle which is broken over the head of one of the burglars in *Charlie Girl*.

In *Jorrocks* Belinda has to change out of her dress into Benjamin's costume while singing 'I don't want to behave like a lady' and it is essential to rehearse this routine in the costumes which will be worn in the show. Similarly, for the final rehearsals of *The Desert Song* the Red Shadow's outfit should be hired to allow the actor to perfect his quick-change routines.

Any stage band or orchestra that forms part of the show, as in *The Great Waltz*, should attend *all* rehearsals from now on, as should any children who, until now, have been called only as required. Sound effects are introduced, although it will not be possible to set sound levels until actually in the theatre.

Honorary or associate members can be invited to provide a small audience at these rehearsals. Though lacking the colour and spectacle afforded by costumes, settings and lighting, rehearsals should prove entertaining to your visitors, and the cast will gain confidence and practice from playing to an audience.

Curtains and calls

At this stage devote time to the important matters of curtains and curtain calls.

The house tabs for a proscenium stage are either drop or draw curtains. Both have advantages and disadvantages. A drop curtain reveals the actor from the feet upwards as it rises, and cuts off the face of the cast first, as it falls. However, it is invariably silent in operation, and the speed of ascent and descent can be varied to suit the mood of the show.

Draw curtains on the other hand are seldom smooth or silent, have a nasty habit of sticking at the most inopportune moments and are difficult to open or close quickly without much billowing, which can cause the collapse of parts of the set. Lighting is often cued to curtains. One method is to start a scene in a blackout, open the curtains and then bring up the lights; alternatively, one can fade in the lighting as the curtain rises or opens and dim them as it falls or closes. The speed of operation is a matter for the director to decide, having regard to the psychological mood of the scene.

Productions staged in the round or the arena stage, with no curtains, will rely entirely on lighting. Thought must be given to whether 'snap' lighting or a gentle fading of the lights is the more appropriate for the show.

Curtain calls should be planned and blocked like other routines. If no music is provided for the calls, the musical director should use a suitable reprise for the purpose; it need not be vocalised, although most scores lend themselves to reprises of the 'hit' numbers from the show. After the finale tableau, audiences may demand further calls and the director should decide whether these are to be taken and how they are to be arranged. The company remains on stage at the end of each performance until dismissed by the stage manager.

The National Anthem

Normal practice is to start the run of the show with 'The Queen', played by the orchestra. On the last night, the performance ends with a choral rendering from the assembled cast on stage; it should be considered as part of the total performance and rehearsed as such.

Final rehearsals should be devoted to the cultivation of smoothness. If time does not permit a period of analysis at the end of each session, the director and musical director write notes for the principals to study before the next rehearsal. With an experienced company it is possible to give instruction during the rehearsal without interrupting the playing. The director may shout 'Watch that straight line!' or 'Fill up the corners!' to the chorus or 'Poor exit – carry on' to a principal, and a well-trained company should be able to register such remarks and adjust accordingly. Once they become accustomed to this method of 'directing from the sidelines', they will keep in character and continue playing while mentally noting the director's instruction, and there should be no loss of smoothness.

It may be suggested that a company becomes stale with constant repetition, but I have yet to see an amateur company that showed signs of over-rehearsal. Unhappily the reverse is only too true. There is, however, the danger that the chorus, in particular, may become bored. To counteract this, one should concentrate on a definite aspect at each rehearsal – at one pay particular attention to diction; at another stress the need for playing to the focal point, or run the show concentrating on speed and attack. The production team must be at their most enthusiastic; so long as the company do not feel that the rehearsal is just another run-through, interest will not pall.

Inevitably there will be some troublesome scenes and these should be rehearsed on nights other than when the full company is called. Even when a show is developing well, one may have an 'off' night. On such occasions I give the company its head, and let them send up the whole production; tension is relaxed and the next rehearsal goes with a swing.

Every scene should be timed and checked against the target time; generally the show will tend to run faster with succeeding rehearsals and final targets will need to be amended. Any erratic timing needs to be investigated to discover the cause and, if necessary, correct it. At these final rehearsals the members of the technical staff will be checking their cue sheets, the proposed lighting intensities, timing the scene changes and amending their notes as necessary.

The 'get-in'

Meticulous pre-planning is of vital importance to an amateur group. A professional company will have a week or more in which to get in the scenery, rig the stage and lighting equipment, focus the lamps and hold lighting, technical, orchestral and full-dress rehearsals followed by 'try-outs'. Amateurs generally have to condense all this into a weekend or less, as the theatre or hall is not available until the close of a Saturday evening performance; yet one is expected to be ready to open on the following Monday night. Amateurs have other jobs to do during the week but are usually ready to work all Saturday night and all day Sunday on the 'get-in' although their enthusiasm can be curbed by unsympathetic caretakers who require premises to be vacated at ten or eleven at night.

When the time arrives for the theatre to be completely turned over to the company, the stage crew, under the direction of the stage manager, swing into action. The scenery and lighting equipment are the two major items involved and it is important to get these into the theatre in a logical manner and to place them where they will be conveniently to hand when required. Delegation is essential at this stage, and with thorough planning, the work should go smoothly. If space allows, electricians and stage crew can work simultaneously on the stage – the electricians rigging on the down-stage lines whilst the crew concentrate on hanging the cloths, borders and french flats on those up-stage. Later the procedure can be reversed.

Where possible, arrange with the management to have scenery, properties, wardrobe and lighting equipment delivered to the theatre during the week prior to dress rehearsal. In addition cultivate the goodwill and co-operation of the resident stage manager and electrician since, when circumstances permit, they can often be persuaded to start rigging in advance.

Make certain that the resident stage manager or electrician is told the number of lanterns to be hung so that each bar can be correctly counterweighted.

Before flying out, check that:

(1) Each lantern is fitted with a bulb and is working correctly.
(2) The lantern is clamped firmly to the barrel and that safety chain is fitted.
(3) There is sufficient slack in the feed cable to permit the lantern to be moved in any direction.
(4) The lantern is positioned roughly in the direction it has to light.
(5) It is fitted with the correct colour medium and any gobo required.
(6) All cables have been checked and are clearly labelled at off-stage ends with their circuit numbers.
(7) Any locking nuts are not so overtightened as to be immovable.

Attention to these details will save time and temper when it comes to focusing. Once rigged and checked, the barrel can be flown well clear of any scenery until ready for focusing.

At the risk of stating the obvious, may I point out that all cloths and borders should have their centres marked — generally with a tie of a distinctive colour. If no such mark can be found, the canvas is folded end to end and the centre determined. This is tied on to the bar or barrel directly under the centre flying line. The piece is then hung, working outwards from the middle. This system ensures that all cloths and borders hang centrally.

Any 'house' tabs, borders and legs not required are flown away or, if their lines are needed, or there is insufficient head room, taken down, packed, labelled and stored until the end of the run. Other unwanted equipment or scenery belonging to the theatre is also packed away. Once the stage lanterns are rigged, the electricians can turn their attention to the front of house lighting while the stage is swept and all old setting marks washed out.

Setting

In a multi-scene show it is a good idea to set in reverse, starting with the last scene and working backwards to finish with Act I scene I standing; the packs of scenery will then be in their correct order and all will be ready for focusing and technical rehearsals.

Once a scene is set, the director with the designer, if any, and the stage manager should check it from all parts of the house; pay attention to the sight-lines, the masking of the openings, and check that borders and cloths hang level. Indicate the 'dead' on each flown piece. When all these points are resolved, mark the set and dress it.

Marking the set involves two operations; the position of the scenery is discreetly indicated on the stage floor at the important points with a touch of water paint or coloured tape. A different colour is used for each setting. Markings need only be big enough to guide the stage crew in positioning the flats — the stage floor need not look like a crazy street guide. The flats are also marked on the back with the act and scene and numbered from the prompt side.

Dressing the set involves placing or fixing all the furniture, drapes, pictures, door furniture and other properties, including decorative light fittings. Again these should be checked and, once their position is agreed, the details marked and noted by the property master.

When all these matters have been finalised to the satisfaction of the

director, one can proceed to the setting and focusing of the lanterns and
the lighting rehearsal. These highly important technical matters will be
dealt with in Chapter 11.

The orchestra

Orchestras fall into three categories: the amateur, the semi-professional
and the professional. School productions will usually be accompanied by
an orchestra made up of talented scholars who, in most cases, will have
been playing together and rehearsing the show over a period of months.
There may be a stiffening of professional or semi-professional adult
players and the orchestra will have ample opportunity to play with the
cast.

Professional or semi-professional players generally make up the pit
orchestra for amateur societies. Sometimes they are members of an
existing group – in years past they could be the resident pit orchestra of
the theatre, augmented as necessary – or they may be musicians who
regularly play for and know the musical director. With the limited time
allowed for an orchestral rehearsal, or band call (three hours), their
technique, discipline and experience are invaluable.

The players in a professional orchestra will belong to the Musicians'
Union who lay down rates and conditions for their members. The
current minimum rates and conditions for members working for
amateur societies in establishments *other* than theatres and cinemas are:

Minimum weekly salary for up to 6 calls	£84.00
Additional performances or rehearsals	£14.00 per call
Maximum duration of performance or rehearsal	3 hours
Overtime on performance or rehearsal	£2.80 per half hour or part thereof.
Porterage	As in the TMA/MU Agreement

THE TMA/MU AGREEMENT

Many societies enjoy the facilities of provincial or suburban theatres
where the management are members of the Theatre Managers' Association (TMA), in which case the orchestras' salary will be subject to an
agreement made between the TMA and the Musicians' Union.

The theatre is duty bound to ensure that only MU members are
engaged and that they will be paid not less than the minimum rate

which is currently £100.00 for up to seven calls. For this sum, which may well increase in 1983, one can expect the players to arrive ten minutes before starting time, play for up to three hours (with a fifteen-minute break) and wear a dark lounge suit or dinner suit as required.

DOUBLING FEE

The MU allows its members to play up to three instruments as required. For payment purposes, some combinations count as one instrument; the flute and piccolo, piano and celeste or organ and celeste are three examples. On the other hand, a trumpeter doubling with flugel horn will cost an additional 25 per cent whilst a clarinettist, also playing saxophone and flute will cost an additional 35 per cent. Percussion instruments fall into four categories:

(1) Drum kit, small effects, 1 tubular bell, 1 timpanum.
(2) Glockenspiel, bells, vibes, xylophone, marimba. (Any three of these.)
(3) Latin American instruments (including castanets, tambourine, maracas, etc).
(4) Timpani (a maximum of four).

HOLIDAYS

Every member of the orchestra is entitled to half a day's holiday for every week that he is employed, but you cannot insist that he takes it unless you employ him for twelve weeks or more. In practice, he gets one-twelfth of his salary added to the weekly wage, i.e. the basic salary plus any extras for doubling, porterage etc.

TRAVEL AND SUBSISTENCE

Should you engage any player who lives more than twenty miles from the theatre, you may be asked to pay for one second-class return rail fare and a minimum subsistence bill of £40.00.

OVERTIME

This is calculated at time and a quarter, paid for each half hour or part thereof. Sunday overtime is double time, paid for each quarter of an hour or part thereof.

PORTERAGE

Certain instruments qualify for porterage, varying according to size of instrument. There are three rates: £5.00, £6.75 and £8.00 per trip, i.e. two trips per engagement. The drum kit counts as one instrument.

TYPICAL BUDGET FOR A 17 PIECE ORCHESTRA AT TMA RATES

8 calls: 2.30 pm Bandcall, Sunday
          7.30 pm Dress Rehearsal, Monday (overran 20 minutes!)
          7.30 pm Performances – Tuesday to Saturday
          2.30 pm Matinee, Saturday

Orchestra comprises 7 strings, 4 saxophones/clarinets etc., 5 brass, 1 percussion. The 4 violinists (no allowance made for additional fee to Leader), the viola player, 2 trumpeters, 2 trombonists and the horn player receive the basic wage calculated as follows:

Minimum weekly salary	£100.00	
Holiday pay	8.33	
Sunday call	28.56	
Overtime	2.98	
	£139.87 x 10 players	£1,398.70

The cellist receives the same plus £10.00 porterage   149.87
The bass player receives the same plus £13.50 porterage   153.37
The wage for the 'doubling' reed players is:

Minimum weekly salary	£100.00	
Doubling fee	35.00	
Holiday pay	11.25	
Sunday call	38.57	
Overtime	4.02	
	£188.84 x 4 players	£755.36

Tenor and baritone sax players receive £10.00 porterage   £20.00
The percussionist, playing kit and accessories plus 2 timps, receives:

Minimum weekly salary	£100.00	
Doubling fee	25.00	
Holiday pay	10.42	
Sunday call	35.71	
Overtime	3.71	
Porterage	32.00	
	206.84	£206.84

TOTAL   £2,684.14

The musical director must establish a close relationship with his players so that the week of the show becomes an enjoyable experience. If he states clearly what he wants, gives a clear beat, and shows that he knows the score, the musicians will respect him and give him their absolute co-operation. A good leader is essential; he is the right arm of the musical director and it is a good plan for him to attend a run-through of the show before band call.

The size and composition of the orchestra will vary from show to show, and one must contact the firm issuing the band parts to find out for which instruments the show is scored. From this information, the musical director can adjust the number of players to fit his budget — always ensuring that the music does not suffer for the sake of economy. The size of the theatre, whether there is an orchestra pit and the acoustics of the building must also be taken into account. With some of the newest shows these considerations are further complicated by the use of multiple musical groups, both in the pit and on-stage, as the following comparisons indicate:

Chu Chin Chow (amateur production)
6 violins, 2 violas, 1 cello, 1 bass, 2 flutes/piccolos, 1 oboe, 2 clarinets, 1 bassoon, 2 horns, 2 trumpets, 2 trombones, 1 percussion, 1 harp, 1 celeste.

A Chorus Line
3 trumpets, 3 trombones, 11 woodwind, 3 percussion, 2 keyboard, 1 harp.

Company
4 violins, 1 cello, 3 trumpets, 1 horn, 5 clarinets, piano, 2 guitars, percussion, drums.

Jesus Christ Superstar
(On-stage): drums/percussion, bass, electrical and acoustic guitars, piano, electric piano, organ, positive organ, tenor sax.
(Off-stage): 4 pianos, 2 organs, Moog synthesizer, drums, 7 guitars, 2 bassoons, 1 clarinet, 2 flutes, percussion, 6 horns, 4 trumpets, 3 trombones.
(Pit): String section.

Certain scores are cross-cued which enables the musical director to dispense with an instrument or two, not from choice but from the expense angle.

Take delivery of the band parts five or six weeks before the band call and mark, in every part, the changes of beat, tempo, cuts and any other adjustments, at the same time checking for any misprints or errors in notation. All markings should be made with a soft pencil and erased immediately after the last performance, as it is unfair to the copyright holders and to the people who will next be using these parts to damage the scores by using a ballpoint pen.

The band call

This is primarily for the musical director and the orchestra. In three brief hours they have to play through the score, checking any wrong notes and agreeing the various tempi, as well as giving attention to interpretation and style. With their experience, professional players will usually take this in their stride.

Before each number the musical director will clarify such points as the number of verses and choruses to be played, cuts (if any) to be observed, which repeats to ignore and whether any encore will be given. He must also state how many beats to the bar will be given; a piece written in $\frac{3}{4}$ time can be beaten either as one or three beats to the bar.

When a new or unfamiliar show is being presented, even a fully professional orchestra may need more than a single rehearsal and the musical director must ascertain this from his earlier studies of the score.

Some conductors like the cast, or at least the principal vocalists, to attend the band call. While attention will be directed chiefly to the musicians, the singers can nevertheless try out their numbers with the orchestra. Unless they are very experienced they will find that the score falls strangely on their ears after being so long accustomed to piano accompaniment. Any vocal problems should not be allowed to intrude on this rehearsal, but dealt with by the musical director at the end of the session. It is not uncommon for the music to be taken at a slightly slower tempo at band call, but the tension and excitement of a performance will soon lift it to its faster tempo.

The arrangement of the players in the orchestra pit varies with individual musical directors. Factors affecting the positioning of the various instruments include the size and shape of the pit, the height of the stage and the instruments for which the show is scored. Consideration must be given to the comfort of the players and adequate space must be allowed to the string players for their bowing and the trombones for their slides. When a piano is called for it is generally situated in the centre of the pit whilst the larger instruments, such as the harp and double bass, which may obstruct the audience's view of the stage, are situated at the extremities. Often no orchestra pit exists, the players being seated on the same level as the audience and in such cases care must be taken to see that the players and their desks offer as little interference as possible with the view of the stage.

The decision on the seating of the orchestra is the musical director's and he should provide the stage manager with a sketch of his requirements so that the pit may be prepared in advance of the band call or the dress rehearsal. In addition he should settle the question of cue lights: whether they are required and what method of signalling should be employed.

If a piano is used on stage during the performance, the stage manager should arrange for it to be tuned to concert pitch for the dress rehearsal, and probably once or twice during the run of the show to ensure that it keeps in tune. Similarly, if a piano is used in the orchestra pit, it will need attention.

The costume parade

Most costume houses will arrange to deliver the wardrobe some days before the dress rehearsal and much time can be saved by devoting one of the last rehearsal sessions to a costume call. If you are fortunate enough to be able to arrange for the principals to have fittings so much the better, but it is proving more and more difficult to fix these.

The costume parade is organised by the wardrobe mistress with her seamstresses in attendance. When the costumes are received they should be issued by the wardrobe mistress and any shortages or misfits reported as soon as possible. The director should see and approve every costume, and a simple procedure is to take the ladies and gentlemen separately, being sure to check the chorus costumes in sets. With the ladies, check fit, sleeve and skirt lengths (it is often possible to let down or take up to get an acceptable matching set of dresses) and pay particular attention to accessories, footwear and hairstyles. When problems of fit occur the expedient of switching costumes around with another player often saves sending back to the costumier for another dress.

Ensure that the men use braces for their trousers, that they adjust their waistcoats, provide collar studs, cuff links and collars where necessary, that their hosiery and footwear is appropriate and, as with the ladies, check hairstyles and accessories. Like the ladies, a change-around of trousers, jackets or waistcoats will often enable everyone to have a passable fit, but it must be admitted that men's costumes are harder to alter and the offending garment may have to be returned for replacement.

When playing a period piece where the men are required to wear tights, ensure that they provide themselves with supports or jock-straps. In one production of this nature I had to give the gentlemen of the chorus these instructions and was asked by a supernumerary, in all innocence 'What about the people with small principal parts?' Needless to say this remark has gone into the archives of that particular society!

If the director is creating a new conception of the show, he should consult the costumier at an early stage to see whether his requirements can be met. Unfortunately many societies ignore this point and merely send in their completed measurement forms three or four weeks before their production. They are then dismayed that the costumier cannot accede to their particular demands. A spokesman for a large costume house once told me that the ideal method was for the director, once he had settled on how he wished to dress a show, to contact the costumier and discuss his plans and, if need be, view the costumes. However, remember that the majority of amateur productions are staged between October and early December and from the start of March through until early May. Consequently any proposed visits should be made in the quieter months of the year.

The accurate measuring of the cast is of vital importance, and all the measurements asked for on the measurement forms should be provided. Women are sometimes a little reticent on this point; it has been known for them to give the measurements that they would like to be, rather than the sizes they really are. One error, frequently made, is that the bra size is given instead of the bust measurement (there can be a consider-able difference).

For large productions, with many changes of costume, the details of what is required for *each person, in each scene* must be stated (this is especially important when the director's requirements differ from the original estimate). It is quite common for measurement forms to be returned to the costumier with only the individual's sizes but no indication of the costumes required. This causes a great deal of unnecessary correspondence, time and trouble for both costumier and society.

The only judge of the suitability of a costume should be the director having seen it under actual stage conditions.

It is normal practice for the costume hampers to be sent to companies by passenger train. Many societies prefer to use road transport and this should be negotiated separately with the costumiers who will, where they can, fall in with such arrangements. One important point: where an arrangement has been made that the costumes will be ready for collection at a given hour on a certain day, it must be adhered to. A costumier may be sending out between ten and thirty productions every week in the busy season; he has to work to very tight schedules, and every hour is important.

Relations between amateur companies and costumiers are not always what they should be and often the fault lies with the company. One of the main causes of friction is the question of makeup on costumes. It is very difficult to understand why many amateurs consider it necessary to apply so much makeup and to a much larger area than do professionals. Even after a long run in the West End, with a possible tour after that run, costumes are not marked to anywhere near the same degree that they are after one week's hire to an amateur society. This has been a problem for many years, and no one has yet been able to find a solution.

A chief cause of stained costumes is the use of fizzy drinks to simulate champagne. These stains cannot be removed and, because of the high cost of costumes, one that has been stained in this manner cannot simply be discarded. It has to be re-hired with the predictable complaint.

When returning costumes the hampers should be packed as far as possible in the same way as they were received. Great care should be taken to see that hats and fragile head-dresses are not packed at the bottom of hampers under heavy boots or swords. If any special instructions were included in the hampers on receipt, they should be observed when packing for return.

Arrangements should have been made for the return of the hampers by road transport or by passenger train and they should be dispatched on the next working day after the last performance. It is sometimes not realised that when costumes are returned by British Rail, they will not actually be put on a train until the carriage charges have been paid. It is not sufficient to ask the railway to collect the skips; this will be done, but the goods will not be dispatched until the carriage has been paid.

Some Acting Editions include a costume plot at the end of the libretto which can be of help. But be careful. I recall the time I ordered double knickers from a costumier for *Annie Get Your Gun* for the women's chorus in Act 2. On being asked what I wanted I pointed out the details in the libretto. (I was not quite certain what these articles of apparel were or why the women should require them.) It was gently pointed out to me that what was meant was that the women's chorus used the same underwear in Act 2 as they did in Act 1 – they doubled them.

The photo-call

Amateurs rarely have time to hold a photo-call, and such photographs as are required are usually taken as and when possible during the dress rehearsal. Luckily there are photographers who specialise in this but, where time allows, a proper photo-call should be arranged. The photographer, with the director, can decide which sections of the show will provide the best shots and a schedule can be drawn up calling the artists required. The pictures do not have to be composed exactly as they are in performance and the director should be advised by the photographer if the latter is an expert. Lighting will need to be modified and the electrician should be in attendance. If time is short, suitable flats can be erected in another part of the theatre and stage floods and spotlights on stands can augment the photographer's lighting equipment. If the subject of the show lends itself, consider exterior shots on location – I have seen excellent studies for *Camelot* shot at Sherborne Castle; *Anne of Green Gables, Oklahoma!* and *Half a Sixpence* are other shows where location work could be used.

The dress rehearsal

Ideally this is run without interruption, as like an actual performance as possible. If, as has been suggested, the director has given due attention to the technical problems in advance, and introduced the special costumes, properties and effects into the rehearsals preceding the dress rehearsal, it should be possible to complete a run-through in three hours or so. If the show is particularly difficult, or is a new one, the first dress rehearsal can be played to piano accompaniment only, when the director can concentrate on the technical problems and stop where necessary to correct or sort out any troubles.

The dress rehearsal is a trial performance and one should allow the show to run through to the end, saving all comments and criticism until then. Sideline coaching can still be used, as can minor alterations of lighting cues and levels – provided that one does not confuse the switchboard operator who is feeling his way through the show.

Once the show is over, allow the musical director to go over any musical problems to avoid keeping the orchestra unduly (especially important if they are members of the Musicians' Union). Then cover any major faults that need re-running and finally give the remainder of the notes, not forgetting to include any of the choreographer, musical director and stage manager. Try to dismiss the company at a reasonable hour and, above all, send them home with a feeling of achievement and a determination to do better on the night. I certainly do not hold with the old adage that a bad dress rehearsal means a good show. With nervousness and the strangeness of their surroundings, some minor mishaps are inevitable, but if the show has major faults at this stage, the fault lies with the director.

[9]

The school production

This chapter is directed at schools with pupils in the 11–18 age-group, whether they are coeducational or not, and although it is hoped that colleges and similar establishments will find some useful advice in this section, in the main their methods of mounting a show will follow those of the amateur companies discussed generally throughout this book.

As long ago as 1921, Granville-Barker was urging the educational claims of acting in schools yet, whilst drama has since been recognised as a useful educational tool, it was not until after the Second World War that it found a place in the curriculum.

In the early 1900s drama was 'relegated to the status of an extraneous and semi-recreational, or even ceremonial, activity. It is possible that most school plays produced for some annual occasion have been selected by a member of the staff with a view to the parent public that is to be pleased than to the pupils who are to be trained,' wrote T.G. Williams around 1930.

Even so, there were many enlightened teachers prepared to give up their free time to produce school shows. The staple diet for the musical productions were the Gilbert and Sullivan operas – even in all-boys' schools where the trebles or boy sopranos played the female roles.

In recent years horizons have broadened to include modern shows which have special appeal for, and are capable of being performed by, children. Noting this trend, many writers have composed musicals specially for the schools' market, while some ambitious establishments have created their own shows, with words and music written by members of the teaching staff, often with the willing collaboration of the pupils. A typical example is *Star Man*, a rock musical, first produced by Yeovil College in 1980.

Drama is now included in the school syllabus as an examination subject at CSE, O- and A-levels. Practical work and written papers are involved and musicals are frequently included in the list of scripts to be studied. *Oh What a Lovely War!* has featured in O-level texts for several years, which accounts for the large number or student productions since drama teachers try to relate the school show to the syllabus.

Another reason for the popularity of the musical as a 'set' piece is that it gives the examinee the opportunity to demonstrate a wider diversity of talents than would a straight play, including as it does, music, singing, mime and movement and ensemble playing.

Departments involved

Properly planned and organised, and given the enthusiastic co-operation of the teaching staff, the school production can be a great unifying project for the whole school. Every department can be usefully involved, both in the mounting of the production and in the educational spin-off.

Consider a presentation of *Cabaret*. The responsibilities of the Music and Drama departments are immediately obvious. The English department could study writers of the 1930s, such as Christopher Isherwood and his contemporaries; British and German social history of the twentieth century would provide valuable background to the text, whilst budgeting, costing and accounting of the production would afford practical exercises for the Mathematics department. Scenery needs to be designed, constructed and painted, properties, furniture and costumes made. An orchestra must be assembled and rehearsed, dancing and movement taught; the lighting of the production affords opportunities for tuition in the use and application of electricity; posters, programmes and tickets require designing and printing while copyright, Police and Fire regulations and other legal matters have to be investigated. Moreover, the school production takes the pupil out of the horizontal stratification required for normal teaching purposes, and involves him in a vertical stratification ranging over all the scholars and staff; the pupil-players are brought into a new relationship with their tutors which may have considerable social value.

First considerations

Having obtained the consent of the headmaster and any governing bodies, it is advisable to seek the approval of the local education authority and ascertain whether the proposed premises are licensed for the public performances of stage plays in accordance with the Theatres Act, 1968. Even should an occasional play licence be necessary, it is probable that the licensing authority will be able to grant a statutory exemption from payment of any fee for a school production. It will, however, be necessary to comply with any duties concerning the safety of children arising under Section 12 (1) of the Children and Young Persons Act 1933.

An early task is to contact the owner of the Performing Rights of any show under consideration to ensure that permission will be granted for the performances to take place. Unless the show is out of copyright, or has been specially written by the school staff and pupils, fees will have to be paid, and failure to obtain permission or pay the appropriate fee could result in heavy damages.

Choice of show

The choice of a show for a school production is of paramount importance, especially if one is seeking to involve all age groups. A large cast, fast action, good rousing choruses with plenty of character parts is what is required. The romantic aspect is best kept to the minimum since many teenagers find difficulty in playing such scenes and are embarrassed by their schoolfellows' reaction to love scenes. In addition, try to avoid those scores which make heavy demands vocally, particularly at the extremes of the voice range.

The venue

Not all schools will possess a stage large enough to accommodate the big cast. In many cases the assembly hall or gymnasium will have to serve as a theatre; it will be devoid of any but the most basic stage equipment, and the director and designer will have to build the show from scratch. C.B. Purdom comments that '. . . the stage provided in the usual school hall should never be used. It is better to use the floor of the hall and not to think about the stage at all.' I would not go as far as Mr Purdom. I have seen the stage used in conjunction with a series of rostra, the latter being stepped to the level of the hall floor, affording a variety of acting areas which were used to great effect. This arrangement had the added advantage of providing several levels enabling a large cast of vastly differing heights to be grouped so that all could be seen by the audience. Occasionally the stage curtains were closed allowing settings to be changed, out of view, while the action continued in other acting areas.

Peter Pan (a new musical version by Piers Chater-Robinson) was first staged in a school gymnasium. The audience was accommodated in tiered seating ranged along the two longest walls while the whole of the central area, together with the stage at one end of the hall and a platform constructed at the other were used as acting areas for the many scenes.

It is unlikely that a school hall will have permanent fixed seating, (certainly none will be found in the gymnasium) and while you will wish to provide as many seats as possible with a good view of the perform-ance, any temporary seating layout requires the approval of the local authority. Excellent guidance on this, and many other matters relating to performances in school halls, is given in *Play Safe* issued by the Greater London Council. Although the conditions discussed apply to premises within the GLC area, they provide valuable data on aspects that must be considered when putting on a public show in school premises.

The production team

The overall direction of the show will fall to a member of the staff; the Drama or English departments should provide a candidate or there may be a teacher, experienced in theatre or involved with a local amateur musical company willing to take on the job. Another possibility is that one of the music instructors would be willing to undertake both direction and musical direction. The amount and the standard and type of dancing will depend both on the show selected and whether one can find a dancing instructor. One might inquire among the P.E. instruc-tors, since they are certain to have some knowledge of movement. After all, one is seeking not complex choreography but simple, well-co-ordinated movements. Do not overlook the fact that many girls in coeducational schools attend ballet classes and it may prove possible to find a talented, older pupil capable of devising and setting the dance routines.

It is only fair to point out that any teacher becoming involved in such a project will be involving themselves with a lot of extra work, most of which, of necessity, will have to be carried on outside class time. All the considerations which affect an amateur company are equally relevant to the school production; the only proviso I might make is that, with a school show, the high standards and polish are not expected to the same degree, *although they should always be aimed for.*

Casting the show

Assembling a company will give few problems; a general announcement at assembly, or a notice on the school notice board will produce more than enough volunteers, although some may be lost after their initial burst of enthusiasm has abated.

An initial task is to sort out the voices and ascertain that all can sing in tune. Should any prove musically unsuitable, it may be possible to allocate them a non-singing part. Otherwise one must tactfully direct their enthusiasm into other channels of the production. It is not essential that every chorus should be harmonised, even if so scored, but some part-singing should be attempted. When teaching musical shows to boys and girls in secondary and grammar schools, Harold Smethurst had 'no hesitation in making minor alterations to the music where it is unsuitable or too difficult'.

In an all-boy cast, the twelve- and thirteen-year-olds will generally supply the trebles; the older boys, whose voices are losing their brightness at the top of the range, being more suited to the alto lines.

Selection of the principals is not so easy. One may opt for auditions, but standards cannot be as strictly applied as they would in an amateur company. Another method is to hold a general reading, giving opportunity for any aspirants to read parts of their choice, and from these make a choice. Yet even here lies a danger. Many people can read excellently, but cannot act and since the opposite is equally true, one may well overlook a talented performer. If the school has a Drama department the problem is solved, since the drama teacher or teachers will be in the best position to advise on the suitability of candidates from their showing in class. Should several performances be planned, and if there are sufficient applicants of suitable standard, parts may be doubled, the actors playing alternate performances.

The scenery

Not every scholar will wish to appear in the show, but many will be eager to be involved with the technical side of the production. Every encouragement should be given to them to undertake jobs supervised by qualified members of the staff.

Scenery made by the school will not only be tailor-made to specific requirements but offers opportunities for many talents. A word of warning: there are conditions and local by-laws relating to the materials, the construction and fireproofing of sets and these must be complied with, especially when staging the show in the round or on a thrust stage. It will be to your advantage to solicit the assistance of the local fire officer in this respect.

Costumes

Few schools will wish to go to the expense of hiring costumes. They are expensive and it is difficult to obtain sets to fit children. Any hiring is best limited to special outfits, those costumes which are difficult to make and the occasional one that may be required for a member of the staff playing in the show.

Oklahoma!, *Calamity Jane* or *West Side Story* should present little difficulty – jeans, brightly coloured shirts and boots for the boys and simple dresses for the girls would form the basic wardrobe. The costumes for the Peer's Chorus in *Iolanthe* might well stretch the ingenuity of the teacher in charge of wardrobe, but on the other hand, *The Wizard of Oz* allows the imagination to run riot and the designs could well be done by the pupils. Should the actual making of them be impractical at school one can usually find sympathetic mothers to lend a hand. However, it would be unfair to expect them to supply all the materials (although it is surprising what they will provide) and provision should be made in the budget for their purchase.

Do not make the costumes too elaborate, bearing in mind that both cast and audience will readily accept the 'make believe' convention, and much can be done by clever suggestion.

Lighting the show

The theory and practice of stage lighting is discussed in detail in Chapter 11. Whilst schools do exist with fully equipped halls, complete with up-to-date lighting systems, the majority will have to improvise with a few basic lanterns plus hired or home-made equipment. Be certain to check the capacity of the mains supply if adding to an existing system. Any work carried out in this department must be under the supervision of a fully qualified member of the staff who should, as with scenery, liaise with the local authorities in matters of safety and fire precautions. Correct loading, wiring, fusing and plugging are of paramount importance and any lanterns placed over the stage or audience must be correctly rigged and have safety chains. Pupils involved with the handling or control of any of the electrical equipment must be warned of the potential dangers inherent in electricity.

The accompaniment

One can of course play safe and perform to piano accompaniment, but with so many talented musicians in schools today it would be a pity not to attempt to use even a small combination of instruments. Members of the music faculty will be the best judges of who should form the orchestra. The teacher conducting may opt to do this from the piano keyboard, but whether he does so or no, a piano is a useful addition to the orchestra since it can fill in for any weak or missing instruments and give added support to the soloists.

Rehearsals and other matters

The time spent in mounting a school show will extend over many weeks, even over a term, since most rehearsals will have to be conducted outside of normal school hours. The design and construction of scenery and costumes and the preparation of the publicity material may be assimilated into class activity, but lunch time and after school sessions will normally be the rule. Rehearsals will rarely extend over an hour. Both staff and pupils have routine school business (marking, home-work, etc,) to contend with and in a progressive school there will always be other social activities vying for their time; nor will the concentration of the younger members in the cast be held over numerous, long sessions. Therefore a timetable is vital, detailing the dates and times of rehearsals and the members of the cast required to attend. Equally important is the detailed preparation of the prompt book and all that has been said earlier in this book regarding this and the general conduct of rehearsals will apply equally to the school show.

The production team must expect to spend more time teaching and explaining the basics of stage work than their amateur society counter-parts. These will include how to stand, how to enter or leave the stage, how to sit down, and how to avoid masking, although establishments having a drama department should find such matters covered in class.

Towards the end of the term, when examinations and studies are completed, the show should be coming together. With the pressure on academic studies reduced it will prove possible to devote part of the school day to a series of run-throughs, using the full company, orchestra, scenery, properties and lighting – the costumes and makeup can wait a little longer. Firm discipline must be maintained from now on as the excitement rises; if one can incorporate a sense of professionalism within the group, the members will impose their own discipline – a method to be preferred. But be certain to have sufficient sympathetic parents or members of staff available to quell high spirits. Call boys, prompters, dressers and makeup artists will be required at the dress rehearsals – the latter can usually be co-opted from a friendly local society if there is no staff member proficient in the art. It is unlikely that any of the pupils will be adept at makeup, but any that are should be encouraged to do their own.

If a professional company is playing the show during the rehearsal period I would recommend a visit by the school cast. It will give them some idea of the standards that can be achieved, introduce many of them to theatre-going and afford an exercise in constructive criticism.

Many schools possess, or have access to, a video recorder. This can prove a valuable teaching aid to both the instructor and the student. For the teacher it affords the opportunity to reflect, at leisure, on the achievements of a class given earlier and assist in the preparation of future rehearsals. In class it can be used to demonstrate to the players their good and bad points. However, the video should be used with discretion, bearing in mind that the techniques required for television acting are not the same as those needed for the public stage.

I would caution making recordings of a public performance, unless the necessary permissions have been obtained – you may be infringing the law, and, in any case, it may not prove practicable to film under stage lighting.

[10]

The stage crew

Good back-stage organisation is essential to the success of any show, and most musicals require a large stage crew. Co-ordinating this team into an efficient working machine is the task of the stage manager. He is the responsible official backstage during the run of the show, the representative of the society, and both the company and the stage staff are responsible to him. During rehearsals, the director has overriding control, but the performances are run by the stage manager.

One hears of occasions when the director is his own stage manager, or when members of the stage staff take part in the performance. In extreme cases I have allowed such things to happen, but the practice is to be deplored. Director and stage crew have their jobs to do during rehearsals and the run of the show, and their energies should be confined to these duties. In an emergency, a director or choreographer may step in to play a role – it is often more convenient to do this rather than a crash course with an understudy or substitute – but this should be the exception rather than the rule.

Stage manager

The stage manager is the director's right-hand man. He needs to be a man of many parts and a devotee of the theatre. Some experience of amateur acting is an asset, and he must certainly be familiar with the mechanics of the stage. He works hand-in-glove with the director, from the first read-through until the final curtain of the last performance.

This involves a lot of detail work and he needs to be methodical and painstaking. The preparation of the master prompt book, the scenic, lighting, property and furniture plots, the various cue sheets and call sheets are his responsibility.

He should attend the majority of staging rehearsals to become thoroughly acquainted with the show and during the performances he is in complete control of the running of the show. He should be calm in times of crisis and capable of making quick decisions have a tactful personality, a sense of drive and the ability to control temperamental artists. He should also be able to delegate responsibility and, above all, to be able to improvise.

During the planning of a production, the stage manager will collaborate with the director on matters of scenery, costumes, properties, and additional lighting and, later, arrange for their delivery and return. He needs a good, practical knowledge of set construction and scene-painting techniques, the functions and rigging of different types of stage lanterns so that he may guide and advise the director.

Stage manager's prompt copy

This is essentially the same as the directors', which was discussed in Chapter 4. During rehearsals he, or the assistant stage manager, will record any variations and this copy then becomes the definitive version of the show. It will contain details of the settings, entrances, exits and business of the actors, the cues for lighting, curtains, music, sound effects and any other data necessary for the smooth technical running of the show. Much is copied from the director's script, but the stage manager's version will embody more technical detail. For example, the director's copy may merely indicate that a scene opens in broad daylight. The stage manager's will give precise details of which lanterns are involved, their intensity and colour. Similar explicit details will be noted regarding the properties, furniture, settings and effects.

Assistant stage manager

To assist him, the stage manager may have one or more assistant stage managers (ASMs). They need not be as experienced as the stage manager and are often trainees. Women frequently undertake this duty. Enthusiasm and utter dependability are the prime requisites. In a large-scale musical it is frequently desirable to have two ASMs, each controlling a side of the stage. They work directly under the stage manager who controls the show from the prompt corner.

Electrician

A theatre will have its own resident electrician, and many halls will have someone 'in charge of the lights' but it is advisable for the company to have its own lighting man. He will work with the resident technician, under the control of the stage manager. With modern control boards, one operator is generally enough, but if working with older equipment, or the lighting plot necessitates subsidiary boards, two or more operators may be needed. In addition, assistants to operate follow spots and to handle lanterns used on the stage will be required.

Sound

With the second half of the twentieth century came the increased use of sound reinforcement in the musical theatre. The improved quality and wide variety of the equipment available today is due, in no small measure, to the demands made on the industry by the growing and highly influential pop groups. We may consider this equipment under three main headings:

GENERAL COMMUNICATIONS
The house telephones linking the various administrative areas in the theatre, including the prompt corner, lighting and sound control rooms, projection box, orchestra pit and front of house.

PERFORMANCE CONTROL
This system will be controlled from the stage manager's desk which is normally situated in the prompt corner (see also bastard prompt). Cueing, whether by signal lights or intercom system, a call system for the artists, warning bells for the bars and foyers and public address system will all be included. An arena production is generally controlled from a sound-proof booth in the auditorium from whence the stage manager can get a clear view of all the acting area and entrances. He listens to a relay of the performance and gives all cues through speaker cue systems to his assistant stage managers who are situated close to all the main entrances.

All of the aforegoing will be found in most theatres and public buildings where live entertainment regularly takes place. In halls where such equipment is not provided it is within the expertise of most amateur companies to provide some temporary system.

SOUND REINFORCEMENT
Equipment under this heading embraces the amplification of music, voices or special effects as part of the performance which is heard by the

audience. Practically every professional musical production today employs some form of sound reinforcement for the actors. The equipment may be fixed microphones located at the front of, or above, the stage; hand mikes, which can be passed from hand to hand as part of the stage business, or individual radio-mikes which allow unhampered movement about the stage. In addition are taped or recorded special effects and amplified electronic instruments, either in the orchestra pit or on-stage.

This is an area for the expert for modern sound equipment is both complex and expensive and equipping a show for sound can add considerably to the overall budget. The choice of suitable apparatus, the layout of the system and the balancing of the sound should be in the hands of an experienced sound engineer. If the company has no qualified member to handle this work the society should consider hiring the services of one of the specialist firms, who will supply both equipment and staff.

Amateurs can rarely obtain or afford the use of the theatre hall to experiment with such matters as sound balance and it is essential that the sound engineer has a good working knowledge of the acoustics of the venue and knows the production. Attendance at rehearsals will assist him to pre-plan much of this work so that, once in the theatre, no valuable time is wasted.

Ideally sound controls should be sited in the auditorium where the operator can hear the sound from the stage at the same quality and intensity as the audience.

Sound reinforcement systems require separate circuits from the stage lighting and attention must be given to the positioning of the cables, amplifiers, speakers and other pieces of equipment to obviate any damage or electrical interference.

Properties and the property master ('props')

The term 'property' embraces every item that is not part of the fixed set, together with everything handled or carried by the actors. The term originated at Drury Lane, when the famous actor-manager, David Garrick, had the words 'Property of the Management' marked on every movable object.

Sometimes a piece of scenery becomes a property, as for example a tree stump or log and, as such, will come under the control of the property master. Properties can be classified under the following headings:

HAND PROPERTIES

The small objects actually handled by the actors on the stage. They include letters, books, fans, wine glasses and the like.

PERSONAL PROPERTIES

These are peculiar to, and are carried by, one individual. Strictly speaking they are costumes; handkerchiefs, rings, snuff boxes, pocket watches and pens would all come into this category.

SET PROPERTIES

The larger elements, more closely related to scenery, but still used by the actors. In this group come the furniture, tree stumps, Tevye's cart, and Sweeney Todd's barber's chair.

DRESS PROPERTIES

Their function is to complete the set, to dress it and give it unity. Pictures, window curtains and pelmets, ornaments, and even certain pieces of furniture not specifically used in the action, can come under this heading.

The responsibility for the design or selection of properties falls to the designer or artistic director, but since few amateur groups boast such a person, the job falls to the property master.

The final approval of the director should be sought on all properties used and this implies that he must have some knowledge of the subject or, at least, sources of such knowledge to which he can readily refer. Whenever possible I prefer to select my own properties. The essential thing is to know the colour scheme of each set so that one can select furniture and furnishings that will be appropriate and not clash with the overall conception. All pieces should be chosen with an eye to their size, suitability and ease of use by the actors; for example, one should not select an elbow chair, however pretty, if the actress using it will be wearing a large hooped crinoline. The greatest care has to be exercised when selecting properties for interiors, and their visual contribution cannot be over-emphasised. Apart from the aptness of the piece historically or nationally, one should consider its rightness for the actual show – 'Is this the sort of furniture that Mr Veit would choose?' or 'Are these the curtains that Gigi's grandmother would have selected?'

Take particular care over the detail of smaller properties, especially when playing in the round. If the show calls for an Austrian newspaper, as for example in *White Horse Inn*, then let it be an Austrian newspaper. It is not difficult to find Continental news-sheets at major newsagents in most of our large cities; failing this, there will surely be somebody in the cast who is visiting the Continent for a holiday, or who has friends living abroad. In the last resort one could write to the editorial offices of the newspaper. Such attention to detail is one of the joys of being a property master. For *Bless the Bride* I have had on loan a copy of *The Times* of 1870 from the archives of that illustrous publication. It was important to obtain one, since the format was different from that of today; the publishers were delighted to assist (and got a credit in the programme) and I had the satisfaction of knowing that the property was correct.

Documents should contain the actual wording, when it is indicated in the script; letters and telegrams should be of the correct size and colour and correctly stamped for the period; flowers should be appropriate for the country and the season of the year. Door fittings (what I refer to as 'door furniture') are seldom supplied by scenic contractors and the provision of appropriately designed door handles and finger plates can greatly enhance the appearance of a set. Electric fittings – wall sconces, candelabra, table lamps and fires are also properties. They are placed on the set by the property master but are connected and maintained by the electrical department. Care should be exercised in the placing of such items to ensure that they do not mask the actors nor direct distractingly bright light into the eyes of the audience.

Firearms

These are often called for in musicals and range from duelling pistols and muzzle loaders to six-shooters and modern hardware. In many cases they have to be practical. Specialist hire firms exist who can supply every form of practical firearm suitable for stage use and most can be hired without the necessity to obtain a firearms certificate, the exception being modern-type automatics. If the show does require such guns, call at your local police station to clarify the current position.

Cover any shots made on stage. Guns have a habit of misfiring during performance and in such an event the actor should retain his aim, keeping his finger on the trigger, whilst the ever-watchful stage manager covers with a shot from the wings. If the stage manager is really on his toes, the audience will be unaware of the mishap.

Repeater rifles play an important part in *Annie Get Your Gun* and I have yet to be involved with a production where one or more have not jammed. To avoid a bad stage gaffe, prepare for such an emergency. Ensure that two additional, loaded guns are on stage during the shooting sequences, and, in the event of a gun jamming, dialogue and business similar to the following is inserted:

ANNIE   Gun's jammed!
BUFFALO BILL Here Annie, take another. (*Hands her another gun. Shooting continues.*)

Early in the production, the director can interrupt the shooting scenes with 'Gun jams!' so that the actors concerned get used to switching to the amended dialogue. Then if, unhappily, a gun does jam during a performance, they will be prepared for the eventuality and most of the audience will accept the interpolation as part of the play.

Flowers

These can be posies, bridal bouquets, vast ornate stage decorations or merely single blooms. On the market there are many varieties of flowers, fashioned from plastic material, which look extremely natural, are cheap and very hard-wearing. Unfortunately, most are inflammable and do not respond to fireproofing. Use them and you stand the risk of their being condemned by the fire inspector. Far better to fashion your own blooms from other materials treated with a fireproofing compound, or buy them through a reputable theatrical supplier.

There is a belief that the use of real flowers on the stage courts bad luck. I believe the real reason is that natural blooms are inclined to wilt under the stage lights, the foliage drops on the floor and may cause an actor or dancer to slip and fall. This no doubt gave rise to the superstition.

Stage meals

Stage food is simple to concoct. If it has to be edible it should be made of something that is easy to cut and eat. Bananas, jelly and blancmange can be shaped and coloured to represent all manner of dishes, require little mastication, and are easily swallowed. In any case the amount of food actually consumed should be kept to the absolute minimum – actors cannot speak and sing with their mouths full. Large joints, chickens, pies, cakes and fruit fashioned from papier mâché or moulded latex can be hired or made by 'props', with any edible portions secreted alongside.

Alcoholic beverages should never be used on the stage. Water, suitably coloured, will serve for most spirits and still wines, while very realistic non-alcoholic stage champagne is now on the market. If a bottle has to be opened on stage, by all means ensure that the cork moves freely, but do not forget to replace the foil cap so that the bottle does appear to be unopened.

Animals

Animals feature frequently in musicals. They come under the heading of properties and should be included on the property list. Specialists who hire stage-trained animals will usually arrange their transport and control. Where possible, try to arrange that the owner is in charge of his animal when it appears on stage and give him ample opportunity to rehearse the beast in the required moves. This should be done on the actual set, under stage lighting conditions, with the orchestra playing if the action so demands, so that the animal can become accustomed to actual playing conditions.

Like humans, some animals can quickly become stage-struck. I recall one delightful donkey used for the duet in *Véronique*. The number was accorded two encores on the opening night, and thereafter the beast refused to leave the stage until the requisite two encores were given.

Many properties are supplied by the scenic contractors and one should ascertain at an early stage which are included in the specifications. Others will have to be made, and the director should indicate through rough sketches, or working drawings, exactly what is required.

The property master needs to be something of an expert scrounger and an inveterate hoarder. If, on occasion, he cannot beg or borrow the necessary prop he, or his assistants, must be able to make it. His guide is the property plot which contains details of the property, its position on stage, or for whom it is intended, and from whence it was obtained. This last detail is important, and I would stress the importance of ensuring that all hired or borrowed articles are returned, undamaged, as soon as possible after the close of the production, with a brief note of thanks.

Fireproofing

Fireproofing requirements can vary from place to place and it is always advisable to confer with the local authority. A simple test for flame resistance is to hang a strip, at least 25 mm (1 in.) wide, of the material to be tested, in a draught-proof place. Apply a naked flame to the centre of the bottom edge for at least 5 seconds. If less than 25 sq. mm has been consumed by flame at the end of one minute, the fireproofing may be regarded as satisfactory.

Effects

Sound effects may be divided into two main groups: those produced manually and those which are recorded on disc or tape. Among the former are door bells, various horns and hooters and off-stage shots. By far the majority of sound effects are obtained from recordings and there is a huge library of recorded sounds available for hire or purchase. Certain firms will supply all the effects for a given show, but it is far more rewarding to make up one's own, mixing and intercutting commercial recordings with manually created sounds until the right effect is achieved.

The positioning of the speaker or speakers for sound effects is very important; the effect must originate from the right direction. The sound of a troupe of horsemen, passing outside an upstage window, may require a series of speakers placed across the back of the stage to achieve a true stereo effect. The same care should be taken with manual effects — the telephone bell should ring by the telephone and not from the wings!

The sound effects cue sheet should indicate the duration of the effect, together with the sound level desired as well as the standby and go cues, and these details will need to be finalised in the actual theatre to obtain the correct balance.

Visual effects cover a vast and complex field and I refer the reader to the Bibliography. Several stock effects — rain, clouds, fire and rainbows can be obtained from lighting specialists. Gobos can also be hired, but it is more satisfactory to create one's own. In the sphere of special effects, the final result will rest with the ingenuity and inventiveness of the effects man.

Prompter

Of all the tasks connected with any stage production, I rate that of the prompter as being the most thankless. It is an extremely important job and, far too often, is given to some unfortunate person at the last moment. Women make the best prompters, but whoever undertakes this position must be capable of sustained concentration. The prompter should attend rehearsals once the director has roughed out the show so that she may be thoroughly conversant with the delivery of the speeches, the pace of the scene and where and when the pauses are intended. Nothing is worse than to get a prompt in the middle of an artistic pause. She will also learn to recognise which of the various actors has a tendency to dry and how to judge the danger signs.

When a prompt proves necessary, it should be given clearly and loudly enough for the actor to pick it up. Give sufficient dialogue – a single word is worse than useless. It does not matter if the audience hears a prompt; the aim is to get the actor back on the script as quickly as possible.

It is difficult to prompt in a vocal number; usually the conductor will supply the lines (although I do know of one artist who carried on singing the alphabet until the lines of the song came back to him.) In the case of concerted numbers, one of the other principals may cover the individual's temporary lapse of memory.

Calls

To enable any production to run smoothly it is essential to keep the stage wings as clear of artists as possible. Calls are therefore vital. They should be given in ample time for the players to reach the stage for their entrances. Calls are made by the call boy – the title applies irrespective of the sex of the individual – and in a large production it is an advantage to have at least two, so that one is always available for any instruction from the stage manager. Call sheets are prepared by the stage manager, the individual calls being marked in his master prompt book. When giving a call, remind the actors of any personal properties they should bring to the stage.

A public address system linking the stage manager with the dressing rooms is a feature of many theatres but this should augment the call boys rather than supersede them.

Stage hands (grips)

These will vary in number and be allocated various duties depending on the size of the production; in some cases they actually appear in the show, as in *Fiddler on the Roof* where changes are made in full view of the audience. (In this case they wear costume and makeup and play as villagers, albeit with very special duties.) Their duties include curtain man, flyman, property men who carry the furniture and, what are called in the USA, grips. Grips handle the scenic units.

When changes are made in a blackout, with the curtain up, the stage crew must wear black or very dark clothing so as not to be visible to the audience and all the stage crew should wear rubber-soled shoes or sneakers.

The stage manager plots the tasks of each member of the stage crew during a scene change on his master work plot. This business is worked out in the same way the director plots the actor's moves. Each grip is then given his own work sheet and changes are rehearsed under the direction of the stage manager. This ensures speedy and efficient changes but it is frequently omitted by amateur companies.

Wardrobe mistress

The wardrobe mistress should be in attendance during all performances, ready to cope with any running repairs, minor alterations and any costumes that may need pressing.

Makeup

From the earliest times until comparatively recently, makeup in the theatre was used chiefly as a disguise. Apart from masks, faces were painted with a variety of pigments, many of them poisonous. Gilt paint was extensively used for gods and there is an account in 1513 of a young, naked child, who was completely gilded to represent *The Golden Age*. (The unfortunate infant succumbed to this treatment shortly afterwards.)

Until the latter half of the nineteenth century, makeup was basically a powder, although sometimes it was combined with a grease or liquid solvent. Indian ink was widely used for lining, beards and moustaches, although burnt cork was sometimes used for the latter, with dire effects. An actor had only to kiss his leading lady to leave visible evidence smeared all over her own whitened countenance.

Ludwig Leichner is credited with the invention of the sticks of grease-paint with which we are familiar today. He was a Wagnerian singer and manufactured these sticks at his home. Fellow opera singers began to use them and in a very short time the demand for them grew so heavy that Leichner decided to set up in business and in 1873 he founded the now world-famous company. Nowadays, water-based makeup has become more popular.

Modern-day theatre makeup is used principally for three reasons: to counteract the bleaching and flattening effect of stage lighting; to assist the actor to appear older or younger; and to assist the actor to assume different national or racial characteristics.

Because a musical is generally performed in a large theatre or hall, utilising a lot of lighting, makeup tends to be heavier than that used for the legitimate drama. How heavy it needs to be will depend on the size of the stage and the auditorium and the intensity of the lighting. Companies playing in the round or arena staging will need to keep theirs closer to that used in a straight play, using only sufficient to restore the natural hues and colours under the stage lighting.

In modern musicals, wigs should be avoided as far as possible; the best effects being obtained with the actor's own hair. When wigs are essential, go for the best. They are costly to make and expensive to hire, but as far as possible, use the finest available. Order wigs well in advance and, whenever practicable, insist on a fitting. Treat wigs with care and always store them on a wig block or mount.

For women, hair-pieces, ringlets, buns and the like will often suffice. Many members will be able to provide their own, but when such items have to be hired ensure that a small sample of the individual's hair is sent to the supplier for accurate colour matching.

Many musical companies engage a professional makeup artist. Nevertheless, it is highly desirable that all members should be capable of applying a competent straight makeup. This greatly eases the burden of the specialist and his assistants who may otherwise have to cope with a cast of upwards of forty or more, when their talents should be reserved for principal and character work.

The director and the makeup artist should decide on the basic shades to be used, and check that the cast achieve some degree of uniformity in their makeup. One does not want individuals appearing with a makeup more suitable for the Covent Garden Ballet — heavily mascarad eyes and white highlights; at the same time, neither does one want the ensemble to be clones — twenty-four look-alikes, each indistinguishable from their neighbour.

Some parts involve a metamorphosis — the leprechaun, Og, gradually becomes mortal and the Senator turns black and later back to white again, in *Finian's Rainbow*. Principals may double roles or, as happens in *The Wizard of Oz*, the chorus play naturalistic or fantastic parts requiring a change of makeup during the run of a performance. The wise director will note such problems well in advance and ensure that such changes can be readily made.

There are no hard-and-fast rules laid down for the application of makeup. Books exist which explain the various techniques, but only constant practice and experiment, judging the results under actual stage lighting conditions, will bring expertise. Help is available from the major theatrical cosmetic houses, who arrange lectures and demonstrations, and the go-ahead society is urged to explore these facilities.

The makeup artist will require a room or secluded corner with sufficient space to lay out his equipment. The makeup chair must be strongly lit, to approximately the intensity of stage lighting – a spare stage flood will suffice – and if the dressing rooms are not equipped with makeup tables, supplementary lighting and mirrors should be provided.

Quick changes

Musicals frequently involve quick costume changes for principals and if no quick-change room is available, a corner of the stage can be screened off to provide a temporary dressing room.

If the production includes dances – and most musicals do – the stage manager should see that resin boxes are provided at both sides of the stage; behind the false proscenium is generally a suitable spot.

Band room

Arrange for a special room to be set aside for the orchestra, where they can retire when not required in the orchestra pit. Ideally this should be situated under the stage, with direct access to the orchestra pit. If space allows, a smaller room may be set aside for the sole use of the musical director.

It is the stage manager's responsibility to see that the orchestra pit is set out to the musical director's requirements, and that sufficient adequately illuminated music stands are available.

[11]

Lighting the show

History

The earliest theatres had to rely on the sun for illumination. Performances were given in the open air − think of the great amphitheatres such as the Colosseum − and continued until dusk. This practice continued up to Elizabethan times − Shakespeare's great Globe Theatre on the South Bank was basically an open-air theatre and plays were given in the afternoon. In the private theatres of the Elizabethan period the distinctive feature was the roofed auditorium but the building was lighted by good-sized windows and daylight was used wherever possible. When artificial light had to be used it was generally candle power in sconces and chandeliers.

There was little one could do by way of regulating light although colour was obtained by filling glasses or bottles with coloured liquids and placing these in front of the light source. Polished barber's basins were used as reflectors to increase the brightness and, later, mirrors and tinsel were used.

Sometimes gauzes were let into the canvas sets and backlit. Initially the entire theatre would be lit with equal brilliance and many were the complaints of eye fatigue caused by the light shining into the viewers' eyes. Gradually, however, the lights were shielded, either by reflectors or by being concealed behind the proscenium arch or sunk in troughs, and more light was directed onto the actors. It was around this time that a trough was used at the front of the stage, and oil lamps or wicks threaded through cork and floating in oil were used to illuminate the scenes − these were the floats and the term is applied to the footlights to the present day.

In the sixteenth and seventeenth centuries one could find the following lighting equipment in a theatre: chandeliers over the stage and auditorium with standing candelabrum; concealed overhead lighting, and side lighting on the stage, including the forerunner of the No. 1

batten; concealed or exposed footlights; a sunken trough, upstage, equivalent to a cyclorama trough, to light the backcloth; concealed, exposed, shaded and coloured lights on the stage.

Gas

The discovery of coal gas was the first important development in stage lighting. It is interesting to read a technical account of the operation of gas lighting on the stage from the 1867 edition of *Chambers's Encyclopaedia*: 'The prompter has command of all the lights of the house. He has a large brass plate in which a number of brass handles are fixed with an index to each marking "high", "low" etc of the lights. And as each system of lights has a separate mainpipe from the prompt corner, each can be managed independently. The proscenium is lighted by a large lustre on each side of the footlights. The latter are sometimes provided with glasses of different colours called mediums which are used to throw a green, red or white light upon the stage. There are gas ladders in the wings and gas battens and these are provided with mediums of blinds of coloured cloth.'

It is not surprising to learn that theatre fires doubled following the introduction of gas – there were 385 between 1801–77. One of the great improvements in lighting, associated with the era of gas was the lime light – this gave a brilliant white light and was extensively used for spotlights and follow spots through to the 1870s. Even today follow spots are still referred to as *limes*.

After a run of over sixty years electricity superseded gas, and the first English theatre to be lit by electricity was the Savoy Theatre in the Strand which was built by D'Oyly Carte for the Gilbert and Sullivan operettas.

Modern theatre practice

The prophets of modern stage lighting are generally acknowledged to be Adolphe Appia and Edward Gordon Craig. Appia found the general illumination produced by rows of battens, striplights and footlights pitifully inadequate, and foretold a new 'form revealing light' – *Gestaltendes Licht* – which would be a three-dimensional moving light which would give objects their natural roundness, shape and significance. Light in nature, broadly speaking, may be divided into two categories – specific, directional light, like the direct rays of the sun, and diffused, general light which is reflected from the atmosphere and light coloured surfaces. These two categories possess four controllable properties: intensity, colour, distribution, and movement.

INTENSITY

This is the brightness of light, which can range from the merest glow to a blaze as bright as the eye can stand. This brightness is subjective; one tiny candle burning on a darkened stage will appear bright to the eye, while a 2 kW spotlight may appear dim on a fully lit stage. As the intensity of light changes, the eye of the observer will adapt itself, so that brightly lit scenes will appear even brighter, by contrast, if they follow a scene which has been dimly lit. It is for this reason that we try to keep the lighting in the auditorium at a fairly low intensity so that, when the curtain rises, the lit stage will appear to be all that much brighter in comparison.

Too much or too little light, and too many rapid changes of intensity can tire the eyes of the observer; the reader has only to think of the effect on the eyes of driving in a fog, strobes at discos or being without sunglasses on a really glaringly bright day.

The amount of brightness, or intensity, needed to allow the audience to see clearly, will depend on the colour, reflective quality, contrast and size of the object being lit, and its distance from the audience. The further that one is seated from the stage, the greater the intensity of light needed on the stage, so, when setting the levels of your lighting, you should view the effect from all parts of the theatre.

Brightness can also effect the mood of the viewer – the brighter the light, the more alert is the audience, and thus bright light is essential for comedy scenes. The eye is invariably attracted to the brightest object in its field of vision.

COLOUR

The second quality of light is colour. Frederick Bentham, the doyen of lighting artists, once wrote: 'That white light is the sensation of viewing several coloured lights simultaneously, and that coloured light is something less than white light, must be firmly fixed in the mind.' He was referring to the breaking up of white light, prismatically, into the spectrum, where the colours visible to the human eye range, imperceptibly, from violet at one end, through to red at the other end. By making use of this knowledge, it is possible to create the impression of white light by mixing the three primary colours – red, blue and green. However, the term 'mixing' refers to the use of three beams of different coloured light, focused, one on the other, upon a neutral surface, in their proper proportions (see Fig. 18):

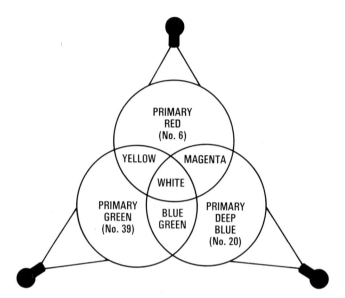

Fig. 18   Additive mixing of the primary colours of light

These three colours are considered the primary colours of light and it will be noted that they differ from the primary colours of pigments. By varying the proportions it is possible to obtain any colour required.

Any two primary colours combined will produce the secondary colours of light: red and blue will give magenta, blue and green give blue-green or cyan, while red and green produce, surprisingly, yellow or amber. These secondary colours, mixed in the right proportions will also result in white light and they can also be mixed to give most other colours.

Each primary light colour is complementary to its opposite secondary colour and correct mixing of these will again result in white light. As an example, yellow with blue = white, since the yellow already contains the red and green light waves. This practice is called additive mixing. It should be noted that colour mixing with the primary colours is relatively inefficient and wasteful of light.

A more usual way of changing the colour of light is by filtering, often referred to as subtractive mixing. Using a primary red medium in a spotlight suppresses the blue and green light waves, allowing only the red waves to come through. Similarly, if we use a primary green filter the red and the blue light waves are suppressed. Use both in one spotlight and no light will emerge since all three primary light waves have been filtered out, yet if we used the two different coloured beams, focused on each other, the result, as we have already noted, would be yellow.

A yellow medium in a lantern will transmit yellow, red and green light; a blue medium will transmit blue, blue-green and green light. Use both filters in one lantern and only the colour common to both will be transmitted – green. We have in fact subtracted the unwanted light waves to achieve the result.

In addition to the visible light in the spectrum it is possible to use ultraviolet light, which is invisible, and used mainly for its effect on paints and fabrics.

Colour mediums are available in three basic types. Gelatine, which is cheap and has a wide range of colour, tends to become brittle and the colours do not last very long; it is rarely used in the United Kingdom having been largely replaced by plastic. This is marketed under several trade names, the most widely known being the Rank Strand Electric 'Cinemoid', and 'Roscolene' and 'Supergel' from Roscolab Ltd. Although more expensive, these are stronger and more heat resistant. Most suppliers will provide, on request, a swatchbook of samples which give names and numbers of colours.

Glass is not widely used in the British theatre. It is expensive, has to be made specially to order, and is difficult to obtain. Its advantage is that it will stand up to long use in very hot instruments.

Some colours tire the eye; we see more clearly the colours in the middle of the spectrum – the yellow and greens – rather than the reds and blues at the ends of the band. Colour also exerts a psychological effect; warm colours and tints are the best for comedy, whilst cool or strong colours indicate tragedy.

DISTRIBUTION

All light has form and direction. Two extreme examples are the thin shaft of intense light from a lighthouse and the soft shadowless diffusion of a misty morning. Distribution varies not only according to the source, but also from hour to hour, season to season and clime to clime.

MOVEMENT

All these three properties can be altered or changed, either quickly or subtly. Natural light is forever changing: the most obvious and dramatic example being a sunset, where every colour in the artist's palette can be in evidence. Indeed, if one attempted to make an exact copy of a sunset on stage, one would be accused of over-exaggeration.

Objectives of stage lighting

VISIBILITY

The obvious use of light on the stage is visibility. Every member of the audience must be able to see clearly those things on the stage *which he is intended to see*. This does not mean that the stage should be, at all times, flooded with light. There will be certain things which they should either not see, or not see so distinctly.

While lighting the actors, one must bear in mind that they move about, and cover all those areas of the stage where any important dialogue or action takes place. It has been said that an actor who cannot be seen, cannot be heard, and whether or not one agrees with this, it is certainly true that audiences rapidly lose interest in something, or someone, which they cannot see.

One actor seldom holds the attention throughout a performance; the emphasis will change, gently or abruptly, to another group of players, and the lighting should underline this change and, in so doing, direct the attention of the audience where the director intends. The follow spot, often used in musicals, is a rather crude example of this technique.

REVELATION OF FORM AND PLAUSIBILITY

One should try to give actors and objects a natural, three-dimensional appearance. To achieve this one must understand that shade and shadows are as important as the light itself. In addition aim for plausibility. The lighting should be a reasonably accurate imitation of the light one would expect to come from the source, be it natural or artificial, apparent or suggested. A sunlit exterior, with the sun's rays coming from stage left, should have brighter lighting from that side, the shadows falling towards stage right. Any arches or doors at stage right will receive the full light of the sun, those on the opposite side being in deep shadow. In a night interior set, illuminated by chandeliers and wall sconces, the lighting should appear to originate from these sources.

COMPOSITION

Composition is the tying together of the stage picture into a meaningful and unified whole. (This is the 'fun' part of stage lighting, but control the urge to create a pretty picture at the expense of visibility.) One may need to add emphasis to some highlights and shadows, subdue less important features and generally blend the light on those areas requiring equal illumination, while still unobtrusively focusing the audience's attention on those areas where the important action takes place. Study of some of the great artists of the past will enhance the reader's understanding of the use of light in composition.

MOOD

This should follow if the former factors – visibility, revelation of form and plausibility and composition – have been properly handled. Possibly the most important aspect to consider, one should never strive for it at the expense of everything else.

The lighting expert, Richard Pilbrow, sums up by stating that the two types of lighting, directional and general, with their four qualities which are used to achieve the objectives discussed above are equally valid for every type of production; it is the content of the show, and the production style chosen by the director, that dictate how they are employed.

Equipment and its function

The lanterns and instruments at our disposal have been designed to give the two kinds of light already discussed – specific, directional light and diffused, general light. The largest, and most useful, group comprises the spotlights of which there are two basic types: the profile and the fresnel spot.

PROFILE SPOTS

Profile spotlights provide a beam of any profile which is determined by the shape of the gate aperture and the use of either built-in shutters or an iris diaphragm. The beam is capable of being brought into hard or soft focus, and most models include a wide and narrow angle option. The narrower the beam angle the greater the intensity of these spots, which are available in sizes from 250 W to 2000 W. They may be powered by ordinary lamps or quartz, tungsten halogen or mercury iodide bulbs.

FRESNEL SPOTS

The fresnel spot has a soft-edged beam, the spread of which is adjusted by the relative positions of lamp and lens. Barn doors may be fitted to trap any stray spread of light. Sizes up to 1000 W are used for general backstage purposes while the larger sizes are usually required for more special effects.

BEAM LIGHTS

These are sometimes known as beam projectors. They give a very narrow and intense beam. However, they are not spotlights but rather narrow angle flood lights. Their usual use is for strong shafts of high intensity light – sunlight through windows, backlighting and crosslighting are typical uses.

PAR LAMPS

PAR lamps are now in general use. In a batten they can be used to skimlight a backcloth and downlight the stage area in front of the cloth at the same time. They are also useful as border or downlights. (Low-voltage PAR lamps are used as aircraft landing lights.)

OTHER LANTERNS

For general, indirect lighting there is a choice of floods, battens, scooplights, groundrows and striplights.

Finally there is the range of effects lanterns – projectors for special effects or scenery; moving effects such as clouds, rain or fire; slide projectors, smoke boxes and moon boxes.

GOBOS

A very useful effect, rarely used by amateurs is the gobo. It needs no special projector and is simply a piece of heat-resistant material, fashioned as a stencil, which is used with a profile spotlight. The gobo is inserted into the gate of the lantern and the effect focused on to any surface. Dappled sunlight through leaves, window silhouettes and clouds are a few of the many effects obtainable from this easily made device. Stock designs can be purchased from specialists.

Automatic colour changing can be incorporated into many of these lanterns and it is now possible to realign and refocus spotlights by remote control. To regulate all this equipment there exist a large variety of dimmer control systems; the very latest, using computer techniques, offer instant memory and visual display units. It would be a very fortunate company that has access to this advanced technology but any director or lighting designer would be well advised to keep abreast of current developments in theatrical lighting; publications such as *Cue* and *Tabs* are excellent organs for this purpose and details will be found in the Bibliography.

Practical matters

Our primary task is to light the actor so as to reveal his features and, at the same time, give a degree of natural modelling to his face. The best results are obtained if we use a spotlight placed at roughly 45° to the side of and 45° above the face. The features take on great character and the expression can be clearly seen, but from one side only. Another, similarly angled, instrument is needed to illuminate the other side of the face; the actor can now move about within the confines of the spotlight's beams and still be reasonably lit.

The space that the cast will occupy and move about in during the performance is the acting area and we must now apply the two-spotlight technique to cover all of this. Depending on the position and pattern of the lantern, a spotlight can generally cover an area of about $2\frac{1}{2}$ m square. Divide up the stage into sections of this size. For easy reference number or letter them working from the prompt side. An average stage divides into 12 of these squares, and to adequately light actors in any of them a minimum of 24 spotlights is required. Those for the downstage areas will be placed over the auditorium on the front-of-house bar, while the middle and upper sections will be covered from the number one and number two spot bars, behind the proscenium.

If both lanterns covering an area are fully lit, the effect will appear flat. This can be counteracted by altering the intensity of one spotlight or by the use of colour. Normally a warm tint is used on one side and a cool one on the other. We can find the reasoning for this in nature; direct sunlight hits the subject from one side with all its warmth and intensity; the other side of the subject receives reflected light from the surroundings and this light will be cooler and of less intensity.

So far, so good, and if we were discussing a one-set show, with no changes from day to night, this set-up would probably suffice. But musicals tend to be multi-scene shows, changing from interior to exterior settings, and encompassing all times of day and night. It is therefore highly likely that we shall have to double-hang each pair of spotlights to enable us to cover all the different situations.

Care must be taken with the positioning and focusing of these lanterns to ensure that the acting areas receive an equal spread of light for actors and audience must not be subject to distracting surges of light as the players move about the stage. Floodlights, fresnels or battens can help to blend and tone with a soft wash of colour, though the floods will usually require hoods or barn-doors fitted to avoid unwanted spill of light.

Our second objective was the revelation of form. Side lighting is particularly helpful in modelling the actors. It should be used from a high angle, to avoid unwanted shadows. Lighting from above and behind halos the actor and helps him to stand out from his surroundings.

Interior scenery need not be specifically lit; it will receive enough illumination from the reflected light of the lanterns already discussed.

Exterior settings are another matter and backcloths or cycloramas need special treatment. They can be lit by battens or banks of floods. The former, using three-colour circuits, provides a good colour mix although the intensity is less than ideal. Floods will provide a better punch of light, but they need a throw of at least 2 m if the ugly cut-off lines from each lantern are to be avoided. A wrap-around cyclorama is best lit from well down-stage to secure the best effect. Depending upon the variety of effects that one wishes to produce on the backcloth or cyc, one may use the three primary colours or rely on a single colour.

Sky cloths painted in analine dye (any landscape painting being in the usual opaque scenic colours) can be backlit — if the stage depth allows. The cloth must be seamless, but the results give a wonderfully translucent effect. Lanterns or battens should be flown very high up behind the cloth and point almost directly down it; PAR lamps are especially useful for this. A strip of plain white canvas hung upstage of the lanterns will reflect any stray light and give added punch. Any landscape detail can be lit from the front by bottom lighting from magazine ground rows or footlight lengths which will need to be masked by scenery or rostra. Ideally these lights should be at least 60 cm from the cloth in order that the colours blend; if they are closer than this, spottiness is likely to occur.

All naturalistic interior and exterior settings will have one or more sources of light — the sun, the moon, electrical fittings, gas lamps, fires, oil lamps, candles and so on. Richard Pilbrow refers to these as motivating light and points out that such sources set the dramatic key of the scene. Once one has established the direction and angle of this 'key light', the other objectives fall into place.

Projected scenery is a practical possibility for amateurs; it is an exciting means of creating backgrounds for numerous scenes quickly and relatively inexpensively. Real or stylised images can be projected on to cycloramas, screens or gauzes, either from the front, sides or behind. This is a field that every director should explore.

The lighting plot – a practical example

We will assume that the director is preparing his own lighting plot. His design starts to take shape as he works on his prompt book; he will formulate ideas as to the time of day, the season of the year, the main sources of illumination in each scene, and these initial thoughts will develop further as the scenic plots are considered. Sometimes the latter will have to be revised to accommodate the lanterns and avoid impossible lighting angles.

Having decided the visual appearance of each scene, the director next decides how to obtain them with the lanterns at his disposal; he starts drawing up the lighting plot. For this he will need a scale plan and elevation of the stage and auditorium, with details of any existing lighting equipment indicated. There are recognised lighting symbols to aid one in this task – those normally used in the UK being the CIE (Commission International d'Éclairage) basic symbols (see Fig. 19) and the Theatre Project's symbols.

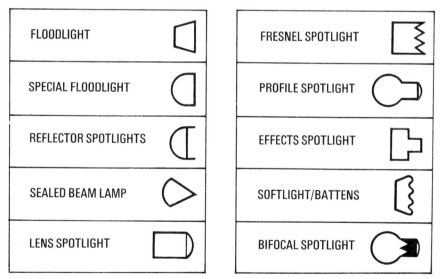

Fig. 19   Luminaires: CIE basic symbols

A *demonstration*

For this I have chosen a production of *The Music Man* which was performed on a town hall stage, since it illustrates many of the problems encountered in an amateur show and demonstrates the use of double-hung spotlights (see Fig. 20).

ABRIDGED SYNOPSIS OF SCENES

Act 1   scene 1 A railway coach: morning
         scene 2 Centre of River City: morning
         scene 3 A street: immediately following
         scene 4 The Paroo house: evening
         scene 5 Madison gymnasium: evening
         scene 6 Madison library: evening
         scene 7 A Street: night
         scene 8 Centre of River City: noon

Act 2   scene 1 Madison gymnasium: evening
         scene 2 Hotel & Paroo porch: evening
         scene 3 Footbridge: evening
         scene 4 A Street: evening
         scene 5 Madison Park: evening
         scene 6 Madison gymnasium: evening

The stage had a permanent proscenium arch measuring 12.2 m (40 ft) wide, 5.5 m (18 ft) high and 5.5 m (18 ft) deep, including a 2.4 m (8 ft) forestage. For large productions, a false proscenium made of drapes, complete with house tabs, is hung level with the edge of the forestage, giving an opening of 11.75 m by 5.5 m. Access to the forestage was limited by the permanent proscenium construction, there was no number 1 spot bar, although an F.O.H. bar exists and some lanterns can be rigged on the number 1 border batten.

The stage area was divided into 12 modules, lettered A–L. Areas A–D were covered by lanterns on the F.O.H. bar; E–H from the number 1 border barrel, and areas I–L from a bar flown centre stage. Backcloth lighting was provided by floods hung upstage.

The scenes played in areas A–D, F and G required both day and night lighting. To avoid rigging two complete sets of spotlights use was made of a 'neutral' colour medium; 36 lavender will appear cool when used with warm tones, such as 2 light amber, and warm when used with a

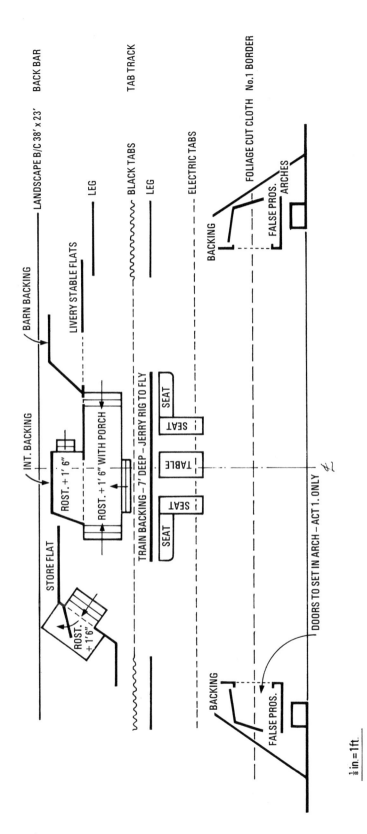

BACK BAR

TAB TRACK

LANDSCAPE B/C 38' x 23'

BLACK TABS

LEG

BARN BACKING

LIVERY STABLE FLATS

LEG

ELECTRIC TABS

INT. BACKING

BACKING

FALSE PROS.

ARCHES

FOLIAGE CUT CLOTH   No.1 BORDER

ROST. +1' 6"

ROST. +1' 6" WITH PORCH

STORE FLAT

ROST. +1'6"

SEAT

SEAT

TABLE

SEAT

SEAT

TRAIN BACKING – 7' DEEP – JERRY RIG TO FLY

BACKING

FALSE PROS.

DOORS TO SET IN ARCH – ACT 1. ONLY

$\frac{1}{8}$ in.=1ft.

Fig. 20 *The Music Man*, Act I, scenes I, 2 and 9: scenic plans

cool tone such as 45 daylight. Using this knowledge, the prompt side of the F.O.H. bar was double hung to cover areas A–D with both warm and cool tones, whilst the OP side carried four spotlights coloured with the lavender medium.

Side lighting presented a problem, but it was found possible to rig spots on booms erected behind the downstage proscenium doors, their beams being directed through the door openings; in addition, space was found on the existing stage switchboard gantry for another two lanterns.

Circuit 30 was used, with leaf gobos, to project moonlight for the ballet and since this was the only time this circuit was used, it could have been 'patched', had there been a shortage of circuits.

We were fortunate in being able to isolate the power from the permanent switchboard and route it through a preset board located in the orchestra pit. This was not the best spot, but it was superior to working blind from the existing gantry. Ideally one would have preferred to site the controls in the balcony or at the back of the stalls.

Focusing the lights

The key to successful lighting is the accurate focusing of each lantern. It is a job which takes time and patience. An expert may expect to take a minimum of two minutes per lantern, which allows one to make a 'guestimate' of how long the focusing of the show will take. Since

THE MUSIC MAN

Lighting Hanging Plot

HORNSEY 1982

NO	LANTERN	POSITION	PURPOSE	LAMP	CINEMOID COLOUR	REMARKS
1	264 Bifocal	F.O.H.	Area A warm	1000	2	
2	264 Bifocal	F.O.H.	Area A cool	1000	45	
3	264 Bifocal	F.O.H.	Area B warm	1000	2	
4	264 Bifocal	F.O.H.	Area B cool	1000	45	
5	264 Bifocal	F.O.H.	Area C warm	1000	2	
6	264 Bifocal	F.O.H.	Area C cool	1000	45	
7	223	F.O.H.	Wash	1000	52	Barn doors
8	264 Bifocal	F.O.H.	Area D warm	1000	2	

NO	LANTERN	POSITION	PURPOSE	LAMP	CINEMOID COLOUR	REMARKS
9	264 Bifocal	F.O.H.	Area D cool	1000	45	
10	264 Bifocal	F.O.H.	Area A W/C	1000	36	
11	264 Bifocal	F.O.H.	Area B W/C	1000	36	
12	264 Bifocal	F.O.H.	Area C W/C	1000	36	
13	264 Bifocal	F.O.H.	Area D W/C	1000	36	
14	263	P.S. Tormentor	X light	1000	Open	
15	263	P.S. Tormentor	Area G/L	1000	52	
16	23	No. 1 Bar	Area F warm	500	52	
17	23	No. 1 Bar	Area F warm	500	52	
18A	123	No. 1 Bar	Downlight B/A	500	Open	Barn doors
18B	123	No. 1 Bar	Downlight C/D	500	Open	Barn doors
19	23	No. 1 Bar	Area G warm	500	52	
20	23	No. 1 Bar	Area E cool	500	17	
21	23	No. 1 Bar	Area H warm	500	52	
22	23	No. 1 Bar	Area F cool	500	17	
23	23	No. 1 Bar	Area H cool	500	17	
24	23	No. 1 Bar	Area G cool	500	17	
25	263	O.P. Tormentor	Area F/I	1000	36	
26	263	O.P Tormentor	X light	1000	45	
27	263	No. 2 Bar	Area J/I warm	500	52	
28	263	No. 2 Bar	Area K/J warm	500	52	
29	263	No. 2 Bar	Area J/I cool	500	17	
30A	23	No. 2 Bar	Area F/A cool	500	17	Leaf gobbo
30B	23	No. 2 Bar	Area G/B cool	500	17	Leaf gobbo
31	123	No. 2 Bar	Area L/K warm	500	52	
32	123	No. 2 Bar	Area J/K cool	500	17	
33	123	No. 2 Bar	Area L/K cool	500	17	
34	263	Stand on elec. platform	X light M/S	1000	45	
35	49	No. 3 Bar	Cyc. lighting	500	6	Pair 39
36	49	No. 3 Bar	Cyc. lighting	500	39	Pair 40
37	123	No. 3 Bar	Backlight J/G cool	500	17	Barn doors
38	49	No. 3 Bar	Cyc. lighting	500	20	Pair 41
39	49	No. 3 Bar	Cyc. lighting	500	6	Pair 35
40	49	No. 3 Bar	Cyc. lighting	500	39	Pair 36
41	49	No. 3 Bar	Cyc. lighting	500	20	Pair 38
42	263	Stand on elec. platform	X light U/S	1000	Open	

2 x Follow spots

Fig. 21 *The Music Man*: lighting hanging plot

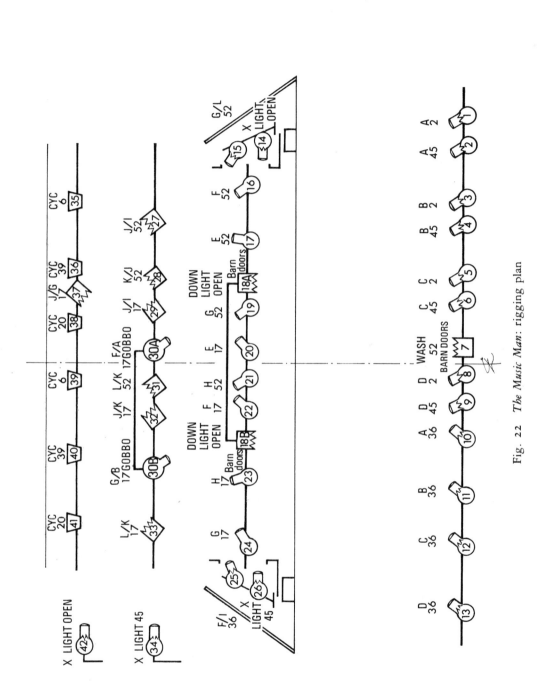

Fig. 22   *The Music Man*: rigging plan

musicals are multi-scene shows, complications can arise. One lantern will often have to serve a number of different purposes in various scenes, whilst another may be required for only one scene. The director or designer should decide which lamps can be focused in which settings, and can, by calculation, be correctly focused for other scenes; and those which must be focused in a specific set.

Begin by setting all the lighting barrels to their predetermined 'dead'. Ensure that the auditorium is completely blacked out, that all working lights are extinguished backstage and that the set itself is 'light-tight'. Then, starting with lantern number 1, work through the rigging plot. One method used for focusing is to stand in the centre of the area to be lit with one's back to the lantern, to avoid being blinded by the light. Direct the operator, by signs, until the centre of the beam is focused on the back of the head – this can be judged by looking at the shadow being cast.

Most spots need to be set so that they blend with the neighbouring lantern, and their edges will have to be soft-focused. Once all the lanterns on a barrel have been set and focused, bring all up to full light and walk about in the areas covered, to ensure that there are no unwanted areas or 'hot spots'.

Lighting rehearsal

A position from the centre stalls or dress circle is a good place to view the stage and some means of communication with the electrician is necessary to avoid having to shout instructions. If exit signs and emergency lighting are normally lit during a performance, these should now be illuminated, as should the orchestra lights, since all will have some effect on the stage picture.

Start from a blackout and check each circuit in sequence, both to see that everything is in working order, and to check the effect that each spotlight is going to give. Then, starting from cue 1, work through the show. As each cue is finalised, have the electrician plot it before proceeding to the next. At the same time an indication of the speed of the change; if necessary, run over the cue a couple of times to make sure that he has understood your instructions (see Fig. 24).

Whilst he is doing this take the opportunity to check the effect from other parts of the auditorium.

It is an advantage to light the show using the actors for, without individuals on the stage, there is a tendency to underlight.

Lighting the arena and thrust stage

So far we have restricted our considerations to lighting a conventional proscenium stage, but many companies and schools are experimenting with alternative forms of staging.

In arena productions, the audience will be seated all round the stage and the actors will make their entrances and exits through them, via the gangways. The stage area is normally smaller but once again we will divide it into the various acting areas. We want to fulfil the objectives discussed earlier and, as before, our principal aim is to light the actors.

In the proscenium theatre the basic method used two spotlights at 45° to the vertical and approximately 45° to either side of the actor. Obviously more instruments are required for theatre in the round. One method is to use three lanterns to cover each acting area, evenly spaced at 120° from one another. More commonly four spotlights are used at 90° from each other. These may be mounted over the stage or over stage and audience. The angles of their throw will have to be varied; those

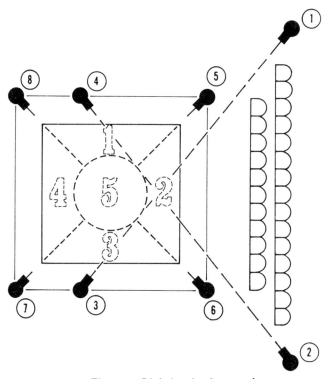

Fig. 23   Lighting in the round

ACT ONE

Pre-set   Sc. 2

$$\frac{4\ 5\ 10\ 11\ 12\ 13\ 15\ 27\ 28}{F} \quad \frac{3}{9}\ \frac{29}{8}\ \frac{8}{6}\ \frac{26}{5}$$

NB: 25 is on throughout the show

CUE NO

5 minutes – cue from SM $\dfrac{6\ 7}{F}$

House Lights
$\dfrac{}{0}$

Overture   As this starts check out slowly $\dfrac{6\ 7}{0}$

Tabs   Score, p. 3, bars 9–12 fade in $\dfrac{5\ 11}{F}$

Q1   Score, p. 5, 'young . . .' fade out $\dfrac{5\ 11}{0}$ fast

Scene 1
Q2   Score, p. 6, fade in: $\dfrac{2\ 3\ 4\ 5\ 8\ 9\ 10\ 11\ 13\ 15}{F}$

Q3   Score, p. 15, bar 3: DBO

Scene 2
Q4   Score, P. 15, $\frac{3}{4}$ bar – fade in Pre-set, with Trailers,

Q5   Lib, p. 7, 'C' min now, Pearl's waiting, Trailers close – check
           $\dfrac{13\ 15\ 26\ 27\ 28}{0}$

Q6   Score, p. 19 – last note of music – Fade to BO

Q7   Score, p. 20 – wait till trailers open on the double bar section –
           Fade in with trailers:
           $$\frac{12}{F}\ \frac{3\ 4}{9}\ \frac{9\ 10\ 14\ 16}{8}\ \frac{8\ 11}{7}\ \frac{2\ 18\ 24}{6}\ \frac{19\ 21}{5}\ \frac{17}{4}\ \frac{5}{3}\ \frac{23\ 30}{8}$$

Fig. 24   *Anne of Green Gables*: specimen lighting cue sheet

from above the audience may require lifting in order to hit the actor's faces, whilst those mounted over the stage may need to be lowered to avoid dazzling the audience seated in the front rows. For the same reason, focusing must be carefully controlled.

It will be noted that these four lanterns do more than our F.O.H. spotlights in the proscenium setting, since they also supply side and back lighting to the actor. Additional instruments may be added for blending, provided that one bears in mind that each lantern will have a varying effect depending on one's viewing point. As there is far less mixing of the different beams of light, colour should be used with discretion. Richard Pilbrow suggests alternate warm and cool tints for the acting area spots.

Lighting a production on the thrust stage, where the audience are seated on three sides, follows a similar pattern; the exception being that the fourth side is usually a scenic wall which may require special attention.

[12]

The opening night and other matters

Backstage procedures vary from company to company, but the following observations are offered as a guide.

The show may run for two or three nights, a week or, in some cases, a fortnight, and although his task is virtually finished, the wise director will continue to keep an eye on things.

Some players take part of their holidays during show week, but the majority of the cast will be at work. They should be encouraged to arrive at the theatre as early as possible – an hour before 'curtain up' is not unreasonable – to allow themselves ample time to get changed, made-up and relax before the performance. Early arrival will also help the makeup artists to prepare the company without unnecessary rush.

Every member of the cast should 'sign in' on arrival; lists are affixed to each dressing room door for this purpose. The call boys can check that all are present when calling the 'half hour' each evening.

The cast, musicians and stage crew must use the stage door when entering a theatre; when playing in a school or hall, entrances for the company and the audience should, wherever possible, be kept separate.

The performances are entirely in the hands of the stage manager. His is a supervisory role and he should not be expected to do any manual work, save in an emergency. In addition to ensuring the smooth technical running of the show, he is responsible for backstage discipline from the whole company at all times. This includes observing the NO SMOKING regulations, maintaining silence in the wings, ensuring that entrances and exits are kept clear and seeing that the cast come to the stage only when called. The stage crew are also his concern. He must encourage them to be on their toes throughout the run, and any slackness on their part must not be tolerated.

A good stage manager takes a pride in the tidiness of his stage; he checks that the house tabs hang well and are maintained in good condition; keeps any visible cables to a minimum and sees that they are neatly laid out.

Members of the cast are never allowed to leave the backstage area in costume or makeup, nor pass through the house curtains to gain access to the theatre, and any 'peeping through the curtain' is strictly prohibited. Visitors may be allowed backstage at the end of a performance only by express permission of the stage manager.

The fire officer

Expect to receive a visit from the local fire officer or his deputy sometime during your sojourn in the theatre. His job is to see that all local fire regulations are being observed, and his co-operation and goodwill should be diplomatically fostered for he has the power to close a show if dissatisfied with any of the existing fire-proofing or fire precautions. In addition to ensuring that all scenery, curtains and properties are correctly treated against fire, make certain that the stage crew know the fire drill and check that adequate fire-fighting equipment is provided, is readily accessible and is regularly maintained. Be certain that dressing rooms contain extinguishers and blankets, and that no unauthorised electrical apparatus, such as electric fires or irons, is used in them. It is a good idea to appoint your own company fire officer to take charge of these matters and liaise with the local officials.

Front of house

The public areas of the theatre or hall are the province of the front of house manager. The box-office staff, stewards, programme sellers, cloakroom attendants, refreshment and bar personnel come under his control. The front of house must be attractive and welcoming; everything possible should be done to give the audience a feeling of 'occasion'. When playing in a school or public hall, extra care should be taken with the external appearance. Posters, boldly displayed at the entrance to the building, should be well illuminated and it is worth installing special lighting to offer a cheerful approach to the venue.

The foyer itself can be decorated in a theme suggested by the show; for example, a circus tent for *Annie Get Your Gun* or *Barnum*. Seating arrangements and cloakrooms clearly signposted and a notice indicating the time that the performance will end will be appreciated by your audience.

Stewards and programme sellers should be easily recognisable as such – evening dress is the usual 'uniform' but some shows do lend themselves to exploiting a theme. *The Belle of New York* or *Guys and Dolls* brings the Salvation Army to mind. There should be enough stewards to usher the audience to their seats, and sufficient programme sellers. The latter should be told whether they have a definite 'pitch' or have a roving commission, and they will require a float of small change. All the staff should be equipped with small pocket torches to assist dealing with latecomers.

It is the house manager's responsibility to greet any dignitaries or special guests invited by the society; each night he should be provided with a list of those expected including any gentlemen of the press. A private retiring room, set aside for the entertaining of these VIPs during the intervals is a valuable asset.

Bells, rung five, three and one minute before the start of each act warn that the curtain is about to rise. In recent years a spoken announcement over the public address system or continuous chimes have been employed as an alternative. Once the house lights have been lowered, one may wish to bar latecomers from taking their seats until the act has started.

The director and the performances

The director's function on opening night is to exude encouragement and enthusiasm. Whatever his personal feelings regarding the show, he must devote his energies to instilling his players with confidence. An occasional reminder may be given, but this is no time for any last-minute changes. As the cast are called to the stage, a cheery 'Good Luck' and then *he should quit the backstage area until the performance is over*.

The hardest task now follows – watching the performance from the front. It is unbecoming for him to be seen in a conspicuous seat, leading the laughter and applause. He should seek a place at the back of the house where he can take notes, quietly and without fuss.

Throughout rehearsals, the director has had to fulfil the function of an audience, anticipating reactions in an objective manner. Now, with an audience watching his work, he may find useful lessons to be learned and implemented. In comedy scenes, for example, laughter may occur at unexpected points, whilst rehearsed laugh lines are received in silence. Timing and pace cannot be polished without audience reaction and, as actors are unable to see or hear themselves, the director's analysis of a performance, and his continual guidance are extremely important. Notes can be made on faults in makeup, lighting or costume, wrong pronunciation and lack of pace.

When giving these notes use the occasion to praise and encourage as far as possible, tempering any criticism with humour and understanding.

Over the week it may be necessary to check any slackness in delivery and reaction on stage, and indiscipline off stage, but a company which takes a pride in its work will rarely require this.

Last night

As the last night approaches guard against a party atmosphere overtaking the performance; the audience have paid to see, and have a right to expect, a polished performance and any celebrations should wait until the curtain.

The final performance can be prolonged by the presentation of bouquets, speeches and votes of thanks; over-extended, these result in an impatient and rapidly diminishing audience, and a restless and embarrassed cast. The solution is to keep all floral tributes to a minimum; allow one each to the leading female players, other flowers and gifts being delivered to the dressing rooms or presented privately once the curtain is down.

Decide how the flowers are to be presented and rehearse the procedure. Keep any curtain speeches, whether made by a member of the cast or the committee, as short as possible. If the production team are expected to take a call, be sure the speaker knows from which side they will make their entrance. Often the musical director prefers to remain in the pit and take his call with the orchestra.

The performance concludes with a sung version of the National Anthem. The stage manager's job does not end with the fall of the curtain. With his staff, he must attend to the dismantling and dispatch of the scenery and lighting, the packing of the costumes, furniture, and properties, ensuring that every item is returned to its rightful owner. The stage must be restored to its original condition; any borders, legs and tabs that were removed for the production must be rehung and everything left in a neat and tidy state. Take trouble over this final task, for such actions endear you to the management and the hiring contractors ensuring that, in any future business, you will receive their fullest co-operation.

Criticism

During the performances the director will have an opportunity to assess his work. For the first time since rehearsals began he can take a more detached view of the production and, inevitably, he will see its strengths and weaknesses. Unfortunately reliable, informed criticism is rarely forthcoming. Audiences for amateur productions tend to be indulgent and receive the good and the mediocre with equal enthusiasm. Few local newspapers employ a drama critic, and any write-up is either done with an eye to circulation or cut indiscriminately by an insensitive editor. So amateur directors and actors seldom get a proper assessment of their efforts which is regrettable, as an honest, fair, critical analysis of the production, accepted in the right spirit, can serve only to improve standards.

Some good, local critics do exist and should be cultivated and NODA and the *Amateur Stage* have experienced reviewers. In many parts of the British Isles, awards are given for the best musical production – the Waterford Festival is one such annual event for amateur musicals which more companies should support. All are instrumental in the improving standards of amateur groups.

Legal matters

Although legal matters are, properly, the responsibility of the business manager and secretary of the company, it behoves a director to be aware of the areas where the law takes an interest in amateur productions. The following is intended only as a broad guide and the reader is directed to the several publications quoted for more detailed information.

LIABILITY AT LAW

Most musical companies or operatic societies with which the director will be working are normally unregistered societies and, in law, 'Member's Clubs'. As such they can neither sue nor be sued as a body, but the members are individually and collectively responsible for the fulfilment of their obligations. Thus members are normally liable for all contracts entered into on their behalf by the Trustees, Management Committee, Secretary, Treasurer or their agents. A director selecting the scenery, costumes, properties, etc, would be well advised to have this selection confirmed by the society or company for whom he is directing. It is worth noting that the members may well be jointly and severally liable if any stranger is injured on premises which they own or which they hire or lease.

THE THEATRES ACT

The Theatres Act 1968 lays down that 'every house or other place of public resort kept for the public performance of stage plays must have the authority of letters patent or a licence'. The three patent theatres in London, which were granted a royal charter by Charles II, are the Theatre Royal, Drury Lane; the Royal Opera House, Covent Garden; and the Theatre Royal, Haymarket.

The County or County Borough Council has the authority to grant licences within its area or it may delegate these powers to a District Council. In the GLC area, the annual licence fees are based on the capacity of the hall and range from £150 (for up to 100 persons) to £9,750 (for over 6000 persons).

Occasional licences are also issued and cover one or more occasions within a calendar month. These range from £50 per day plus £10 for every additional day for a capacity of 300, to £675 per day plus £135 for each additional day for 5001–10,000 persons. However, where the entertainment provided is for 'a Charitable or like purpose', the fee can be completely waived. Therefore, if the Dramatic or Musical Society is a registered charity, and the entertainment is to benefit the funds of that Society, the Council could waive the fee payable. Since NODA is a registered charity, it would seem that a society affiliated to NODA could claim exemption as a charity. Even where the society is not a registered charity it is still possible to seek a nominal fee.

The GLC also grants exemption where the entertainment is, in the opinion of the Council, 'of an educational or other like character' although there is at present no definition of the term 'educational'.

SAFETY PRECAUTIONS

These vary from area to area and, in the words of a NODA spokesman, 'constitute a very grey area'. Whilst rather out of date, the *Manual of Safety Precautions in Theatres and other places of Public Entertainment*, issued by the Home Office in 1934, makes interesting reading. More up to date and comprehensive is the GLC's *Rules of Management* and, together these documents are used by many authorities as the basis for their regulations, although interpretations vary widely from one area to another.

A valuable publication is *Play Safe*, published by the GLC. Although intended for performances within its area of jurisdiction, this booklet covers in clear, concise prose the choice of premises, use of school halls, seating, the stage, scenery, properties, stage effects, dressing rooms, lighting, fire appliances and firemen, smoking and management.

PUBLIC PERFORMANCES

What constitutes a public performance is not easy to define. *'If the performance is of a purely domestic character, held in a private house and restricted solely to the promoter's own guests, no licence would be required, but directly there is any element of a public nature, it comes within the mischief of the Law.'* (NODA *Amateur Theatre Handbook*, 1972.)

Even when admission is by invitation only and without payment, it has been ruled a public performance, and the taking of a voluntary collection for charity would render it advisable to apply for a licence.

COPYRIGHT

We have already touched upon this subject elsewhere in this volume. However, it must be stressed that the usual licence issued by the rights-holders to companies grants permission only for a specified number of stage performances of the work *in its entirety*. The interpolation of additional musical numbers, lyrics or dialogue or the alteration, elimination or substitution of portions of the work, without consent, would constitute an infringement of copyright.

Distinct from the Performing Rights is mechanical copyright. Normally the author or composer will have reserved these rights, which cover recording on tape or disc and filming or video-taping. Before embarking on any of these activities, even if intended for private use, societies or members should obtain the necessary permit from the Mechanical-Copyright Protection Society who act as agents for the majority of writers and composers.

When the entertainment is a public concert consisting of various songs, musical items, selections from shows etc, one has to deal with the Performing Right Society. Many theatres and halls will hold a general licence issued by the Society, but it is as well to check this before embarking on a concert and, where necessary, make application to the PRS or, if affiliated to NODA, to the Director of the Association who can advise on the steps to be taken.

Occasionally gramophone records are played in shows or as interval or 'foyer' music. No public performance of records can be given without first obtaining a licence. The rights of the majority of gramophone records are controlled by Phonographic Performances Limited. Sound effects recordings are exempt, the right to perform in public being conferred on the purchaser.

CHILDREN ON THE STAGE

The relevant act is the Children and Young Persons Act 1963 and full details are laid down in Statutory Instrument 1968 No. 1728 Children and Young Persons, The Children (Performances) Regulations 1968 (HMSO). There is a guide to these regulations – *The Law on Performances by Children* (HMSO, 1968).

From Section 37 (3) of the Act it would appear that no licence is required for up to four performances by a child who has not reached school leaving age if *'in the six months preceding the performances he has not taken part in other performances to which this section applies on more than three days'*.

A child may take part in more than four performances in any period of six months if the performance is given *'by a School (within the meaning of the Education Act 1944 or the Education (Scotland) Act 1962) or by a body of persons approved for the purposes of this section by the Secretary of State, or by the local authority in whose area the performance takes place, and no payment in respect of the child's taking part in the performance is made whether to him or to any person, except for defraying expenses.'* (Section 37 (3) b of the Act.)

This exemption, states *The Law on Performances by Children*, was obviously intended by Parliament to include such bodies as amateur operatic or dramatic societies. The phrase regarding payment means that there should be no question of payment or consideration to procure the child's services and a company that puts on performances with the express purpose of raising money or engages a professional production team is not necessarily outside the scope of this exemption. Application for exemption should be made to the Town Clerk of the local authority in whose area the performances are to take place, or to such other person as has been delegated to deal with such applications.

If exemption is not granted it will be necessary to apply for a licence and this is normally made to the local Education Authority in whose area the child lives. Usually the parents' and head teacher's permission will be required and it may be necessary to secure a medical report.

Children should perform on not more than six days out of every seven, and, where two performances are given on one day, there should be an interval of at least one and a half hours between the child's last appearance in the first performance and his first appearance in the second.

Children may remain at the place of performance for not more than thirty minutes after their last appearance and, if under 13, should quit the premises by 10 o'clock or 10.30 if over 13. If the production is such that they are required beyond these times, they may, in such circumstances be allowed to remain until 11 o'clock. For complete details of this involved legislation the reader is referred to the Act and Statutory Instrument.

FIREARMS

The Firearms Act 1937, Section 4 (10) provides: '*A person taking part in a theatrical performance or any rehearsal thereof . . . may, without holding a certificate, have a firearm in his possession during and for the purposes of the performance, rehearsal or production.*'

However, the person who purchases or acquires the said firearms, or who has charge of them when not exactly in use, must hold a firearms certificate. Usually this person is the stage manager and he should apply to his local Police Station for the necessary document. In recent years there has been some difficulty in obtaining a certificate but I understand that matters have improved of late. The actual weapons used should be hired from the specialist suppliers and details of some of these will be found in the appendix.

UNIFORMS ON THE STAGE

It is illegal to wear an exact replica of any military, naval, air force or police uniform in a stage presentation (c.f. the Uniforms Act 1894 and the Police Act 1919). This injunction is overcome by making slight deviations to the actual uniform in the matter of buttons, badges and so forth.

FIRE PROOFING

An important condition relating to the licensing of theatres, halls and other places of public performance is that all scenery, properties, etc, used in the performance are adequately fire proofed. It is therefore in the interest of any company that hires scenery to obtain, in advance, the guarantee of the contractor that the scenery supplied will be in such condition as would satisfy the local Fire Authority. Particular attention should be paid to any scenery or properties used in an open stage production.

The GLC give two solutions which have been found acceptable:

(1) For scenery and coarse fabrics:

Boric acid	475g (15 oz)
Sodium Phosphate	300g (10 oz)
Water	5 l (1 gal)

(2) For scenery and more delicate fabrics:

Borax	300 g (10 oz)
Boracic acid	250 g (8 oz)
Water	5 l (1 gal)

There are several other legal matters with which the secretary or business manager should be acquainted including Registration as a Charity, Income Tax, Value Added Tax, Lotteries and Play Readings and these are well covered in the NODA *Amateur Theatre Handbook* (1972).

APPENDIX I

Rules of a Society

As an example, I am quoting from the Rules of the Wood Green Operatic Society (1981).

A TITLE

The Society shall be called 'The Wood Green Operatic Society'.

B AIMS AND OBJECTIVES

(1) The objectives of the Society shall be the cultivation of the arts of Music and Drama, particularly among the young of the district and the encouragement of public appreciation of these arts.

(2) The funds of the Society shall be applied solely to the stated objectives of the Society and for Charitable and Philanthropic purposes.

(3) In the event of the dissolution of the Society the remaining funds shall be devoted to objectives similar to those of the Society or for other purposes approved by the Commissioners of Customs and Excise.

(4) At all times members of the Society are jointly and severally responsible for the debts of the Society.

C MANAGEMENT

(1) The Officers of the Society shall consist of President, Vice-Presidents, Business Manager, Treasurer, Secretary and Publicity Manager, all of whom shall be elected annually and all of whom shall have power to vote. The Social Committee Secretary, Honorary Members' Secretary, Members' Secretary, Ticket Secretary and Auditors shall also be elected annually but shall not have power to vote by virtue of the office.

(2) The business of the Society shall be vested in a Committee of members to be known as the General Management Committee, consisting of the Business Manager, Treasurer, Secretary, Publicity Manager, Members' Secretary and four other members, with power to add to their number, five to form a quorum. The Chairman of the

General Management Committee shall be a member of that body and appointed by it. The four elected members shall each serve for two years, two to be elected each year.

(3) Any member of the General Management Committee being absent from three consecutive Committee meetings without giving a satisfactory reason shall be compelled to resign and the vacancy shall be filled by the General Management Committee. No member serving on the General Management Committee of any other Operatic Society shall be eligible for election to the General Management Committee.

(4) The General Management Committee shall have power to appoint sub-committees as they deem necessary. The decisions of any sub-committee shall be subject to the approval of the General Management Committee.

(5) The Social Committee shall consist of a Chairman, Secretary and five other members and they shall be responsible for the Social Activities of the Society. The Chairman of the Social Committee shall be a member of the General Management Committee and be appointed by that body. The five Social Committee members shall be elected at the Annual General Meeting. The Social Committee shall keep its own accounts, which shall be submitted to the Auditors, but shall not incur any liability in the name of the Society without the sanction of the General Management Committee. The Social Committee may fill any casual vacancy or co-opt other members.

(6) The General Management Committee shall publish a brief synopsis of Committee Meetings on request from any member of the Society.

D MEMBERSHIP

(1) Active Membership. Applications for admission to Active Membership shall be dealt with by the General Management Committee. New members shall not be eligible to audition for principal parts until they have completed one show following admission.

(2) Dancing Membership. The General Management Committee shall appoint a special committee, consisting of such persons as they may think suitable, for the selection of dancers for the dancing register. Only members of the dancing register shall be eligible to audition for the Dancing team in any show.

(3) Associate Membership. The General Management Committee shall have power to appoint Associate Members for such period as they think fit. Such Associate Members shall have the same status as Active

Members but shall not be entitled to take part in any production, except at the invitation of the General Management Committee.

(4) Honorary Membership. Honorary Members may be admitted to the Society at the discretion of the General Management Committee. Honorary Members shall be entitled to vote on any matter other than those pertaining to shows.

(5) Life Membership. The General Management Committee shall have power to appoint Life Members. Such Life Members shall have the same status as Active Members but shall not be entitled to take part in any production except at the invitation of the General Management Committee.

(6) No Member of the Society shall receive payment directly or indirectly for services to the Society or for other than legitimate expenses incurred in its work.

E PRODUCTIONS

(1) The General Management Committee shall select twice a year, a group of three feasible shows, which shall be put before the company. One show from each group shall be selected for production in Spring and Autumn respectively. Each selected show must receive more than 50% of the votes cast in its group. The General Management Committee shall provide in advance, each Active, Associate and Life Member of the Company a synopsis and estimated cost of the shows in each group. Only those Active, Associate and Life Members present at the selection meeting shall be allowed to vote. Proxy votes or those submitted in any other form will be automatically excluded. A quorum at the selection meeting shall consist of thirty members, Active, Associate or Life or 75% of the combined Active, Associate and Life Membership, whichever be the smaller.

(2) The General Management Committee shall appoint a Producer, Musical Director and Choreographer for each production where applicable.

(3) The cast for any production shall be selected by a Selection Committee which shall consist of:

The Chairman of the General Management Committee, who shall be the Chairman of the Selection Committee and shall exercise only a casting vote.

Two persons, other than Active Members, selected by the General Management Committee for their knowledge and experience.

One member of the General Management Committee elected by that Committee.

Two Active Members elected by the members of the Society.

The Producer, Musical Director and Choreographer, where applicable. Five members of the selection committee shall form a quorum. The Secretary shall attend ex-officio. The General Management Committee shall have power to fill any parts not cast by the Selection Committee; to revise the cast from time to time, if any member to whom a part has been assigned shall, in its opinion, prove unsuitable for the part; and to re-cast any part becoming vacant for any reason whatsoever.

(4) Members shall attend the authentic rehearsals of the Society punctually and regularly and any member disregarding this rule may be withdrawn from the production, after caution by the General Management Committee.

(5) Rehearsals shall be held on every Monday and Thursday at 7.30 p.m. promptly at Bounds Green School, or at such other times and places as the General Management Committee shall deem advisable.

(6) Members taking tickets for productions are responsible for payment, if such tickets are not returned to the Ticket Secretary at least seven days prior to the first performance.

(7) A statement showing the financial result of the production shall be prepared and presented to the Society not later than one month after each production.

F   MEETINGS

(1) An Annual General Meeting shall be held as soon as possible after 31 May each year.

(2) An Extra-ordinary General Meeting of the Society may be called at any time at the discretion of the General Management Committee by giving seven days' notice to the members of the Society. Such meeting shall also be called within twenty-one days from receipt, by the Secretary, of a requisition signed by at least twelve Active Members of the Society. Any such requisition shall specify the business for which the meeting is to be convened and no other business shall be transacted at that meeting.

No business other than the formal adjournment of the meeting shall be transacted at any General Meeting unless a quorum is present and such quorum shall consist of not fewer than 20 persons present and entitled to vote.

(4) All resolutions to be moved at a General Meeting shall be sent to the Secretary, together with the name of the Proposer at least twenty-one days before the meeting.

(5) All new rules and amendments to rules must be accepted by two-thirds of those attending the meeting and entitled to vote, before they can be incorporated into the Society's rules.

G FINANCE

(1) The annual subscription for the ensuing year shall be recommended to the Annual General Meeting by the retiring General Management Committee. Every member shall pay the sum approved in full by 1 September each year.

(2) Any Active Member failing to pay his or her subscription shall forfeit membership to the Society, except at the discretion of the General Management Committee.

(3) Persons admitted for their dancing ability only shall pay such subscription as the General Management Committee shall decide.

(4) Honorary Members shall pay an Annual Subscription of £2, due on 1 June each year and they shall be entitled to a rebate of 25 pence on one ticket for each operatic production, provided the Annual Subscription is paid before the date of the first show.

(5) Associate and Life Members shall not be required to pay an Annual Subscription.

(6) Members shall provide their own music and libretto for each show.

(7) Accounts for the financial year ended 31 May in each year shall be prepared, audited and presented to the Society at the Annual General Meeting.

(8) Any Active Member unable to participate in two or more consecutive shows may, at the discretion of the General Management Committee retain Active Membership by paying a holding subscription of one quarter the current Active Membership subscription for each two shows missed. On re-entry to full Active Membership a full Active Membership subscription will become due, less any amount already paid by way of holding subscription for the current financial year.

H CONCLUSION

Any matter not provided for in the foregoing rules shall be left to the discretion of the General Management Committee.

Directory of shows, suppliers and services

Part A is a comprehensive list of musicals and musical days which are, or have been, available for amateur performances. These are listed alphabetically by title with the names of the rights' holders or their agents, wherever known.

Title	Copyright owners (or controllers of performing rights)	Title	Copyright owners (or controllers of performing rights)
After the Ball	French	Belinda Fair	French
Allegro	Chappell	Belle Hélène, La	Weinberger
Amasis	Cramer	Belle of Brittany, The	French
And So To Bed	French	Belle of New York, The	French
Annabelle Broom	Weinberger	Bells are Ringing, The	Chappell
Anne of Green Gables	French	Bells of Corneville, The	Chappell
Annie	Littler	Berlin to Broadway	Weinberger
Annie Get Your Gun	Littler	Betty	Littler
Annie Protheroe	Madgwick	Big Al	French
Anyone Can Whistle	Weinberger	Biograph Girl, The	French
Anything Goes	French	Birdseller, The	Weinberger
Applause	Musicscope	Bitter Sweet	French
Apple Tree	Weinberger	Bless the Bride	French
Arcadians, The	French	Blossom Time	French
Archy and Mehitabel	Weinberger	Blue for a Boy	Littler
At the Silver Swann	French	Blue Moon, The	French
		Bluebeard	Chappell
Babes in Arms	Chappell	Bob's Your Uncle	French
Bad Day at Black Frog Creek	French	Bohemian Girl, The	Richmond
Baker Street	Musicscope	Bonanza	French
Balalaika	French	Boston Baked Beans	Chappell
Beautiful Helen of Troy	Belwin Mills	Boy, The	Littler
Beggar's Opera, The	Chappell	Boy Friend, The	French
Beggar Student, The	Weinberger	Boys from Syracuse, The	Chappell
		Brigadoon	Chappell

Title	Copyright owners (or controllers of performing rights)	Title	Copyright owners (or controllers of performing rights)
Brother's Ruin	Clevedon	Country Girl, A	Littler
Buccaneer, The	French	Cowardy Custard	French
Bye Bye Birdie	Musicscope	Cox and Box	No performing fee
		Curse of the Werewolf, The	French
Cabaret	Musicscope		
Cabaret Girl, The	Littler		
Calamity Jane	Weinberger	Dairymaids, The	French
Call it Love	French	Damask Rose	French
Call Me Madam	Chappell	Dames at Sea	French
Camelot	Chappell	Damn Yankees	Weinberger
Can-Can	Musicscope	Dancing Mistress, The	Littler
Candide	Weinberger	Dancing Years, The	French
Card, The	Weinberger	Daughter of the Regiment	Boosey & Hawkes
Careless Rapture	French	Dazzle	Musicscope
Carissima	French	Dear Miss Phoebe	Littler
Carmen	Cramer	Deluded Bridegroom, The	Chappell
Carousel	Chappell	Desert Song, The	French
Castles in Spain	French	Desert Wings	NODA
Catherine	Littler	Destry Rides Again	Musicscope
Cavalcade	French	Dick Turpin	Weinberger
Celebration	Weinberger	Dirty Bertie	French
Charlie Girl	Chappell	Divorce Me, Darling	French
Chicago	French	Do I Hear a Waltz?	Chappell
Chinese Honeymoon, A	Littler	Dogs of Devon	Curwen
Chocolate Soldier, The	Weinberger	Dollar Princess, The	Weinberger
Christmas Carol, A	French	Don't be beastly Mr Dracula	Richmond
Christopher Columbus	Weinberger		
Chrysanthemum	French	Dorothy	Chappell
Chu Chin Chow	French	Dracula Spectacular	French
Cinderella	Chappell	Drunkard, The	Weinberger
Cindy	Musicscope	DuBarry, The	French
Cinema Star	French	Duchess of Dantzig, The	Littler
Cingalee, The	Littler	Duenna, The	French
Circus Girl, The	Littler		
Cole	French	Earl and the Girl, The	French
Company	Weinberger	Emerald Isle, The	Chappell
Conspirators, The	Chappell	Engaged	Chappell
Count of Luxembourg, The	Glocken Verlag	England, our England	French
Count of Luxembourg, The (Hood/Ross version)	Littler	Ernest in Love	Weinberger
		Expresso Bongo	French

Title	Copyright owners (or controllers of performing rights)	Title	Copyright owners (or controllers of performing rights)
Fade In, Fade Out	Musicscope	Going Greek	NODA
Fantasticks, The	Weinberger	Golden City	Richmond
Fiddler on the Roof	Chappell	Golden Moth, The	Littler
Fings Ain't Wot They		Gondoliers, The	No performing fee
Used To Be	French	Good Companions, The	Chappell
Finian's Rainbow	Chappell	Goodnight Vienna	French
Fledermaus, Die	Weinberger	Grab Me a Gondola	Littler
Floradora	NODA	Grand Duchess, The	Weinberger
Flower Drum Song	Chappell	Grand Duke, The	No performing fee
Follies	Weinberger	Grand Tour	French
Follow That Girl	French	Grease	French
Follow the Star	Chappell	Great American Backstage	
Fosdyke Saga	French	Musical, The	French
Fountain of Youth	Elkin/Novello	Great Waltz, The	Musicscope
Frederica	Glocken Verlag	Greek Slave, A	Littler
Free As Air	French	Guys and Dolls	Weinberger
Funny Face	French	Gypsy	Musicscope
Funny Girl	Musicscope		
Funny Thing Happened		Haddon Hall	No performing fee
on the Way		Hair	Musicscope
to the Forum, A	Weinberger	Half a Sixpence	Chappell
		Half in Earnest	Chappell
Gaiety Girl, A	NODA	Harmony Hill	NODA
Gay's the Word	French	Havana	Littler
Geisha, The	Littler	Helen Come Home	French
George M	Musicscope	Hello Dolly!	Musicscope
Gigi	Musicscope	Here's A How De Do	NODA
Gipsy Baron, The	Weinberger	High Button Shoes	Musicscope
Gipsy Fiddler	NODA	Hit the Deck	French
Gipsy Love	Glocken Verlag	HMS Pinafore	No performing fee
Gipsy Love		How to Succeed in Business	
(Hood/Ross Version)	Littler	Without Really Trying	Weinberger
Gipsy Princess, The	Weinberger	Huckleberry Finn	Richmond
Girl Behind the Counter,		Hugh the Drover	Curwen
The	NODA		
Girl Crazy	French	I Do, I Do	Weinberger
Girl Friend, The	French	I Married an Angel	Chappell
Girl from Utah, The	Littler	I'm Getting My Act	
Girls of Gottenburg, The	Littler	Together and	
Glamorous Night	French	Taking it on the Road	French
Godspell	French	Inn of the Sixth	
		Happiness, The	Richmond

Title	Copyright owners (or controllers of performing rights)	Title	Copyright owners (or controllers of performing rights)
Iolanthe	No performing fee	Love at the Inn	Aschelberg
Irene	Musicscope	Love from Judy	Littler
Irma La Douce	French		
Ivanhoe		Mack and Mabel	French
		Madame Pompadour	Littler
Jack and the Beanstalk	Weinberger	Magyar Melody	French
Jack the Ripper	French	Maid of the Mountains, The	Littler
Jacques Brel is Alive and Well	Weinberger	Make me an Offer	Littler
Jennings Abounding!	French	Mame	Musicscope
Jill Darling!	French	Man of La Mancha, The	Musicscope
Jolly Roger	Boosey & Hawkes	Maritza	Weinberger
Jorrocks	Chappell	Marriage Market, The	Littler
		Masquerade	French
Katinka	French	Matchgirls, The	French
King and I, The	Chappell	Me and Juliet	Chappell
King's Rhapsody	French	Me and My Girl	French
Kismet	French	Meet Me by Moonlight	French
Kiss Me Kate	Musicscope	Mercenary Mary	French
Kitty Grey	Littler	Merrie England	Chappell
		Merry Widow, The	Glocken Verlag
Lady Be Good!	French	Mikado, The	No performing fee
Lady Madcap	Littler	Miss Hook of Holland	Littler
Lady of the Rose, The	Littler	Mr Cinders	French
Land of Smiles, The	Glocken Verlag	Mr Pepys	Cramer
Last Waltz, The	Littler	Monsieur Beaucaire	Ascherberg
Liberty Beat	French	Most Happy Fella, The	Weinberger
Lilac Domino, The	French	Moulin Rouge	Richmond
Lilac Time	Weinberger	Mountebanks, The	D'Oyly Carte
Lily of Killarney	No performing fee	Mousmé, The	French
Lisa	Weinberger	Music in the Air	Chappell
Lisbon Story, The	Chappell	Music Man, The	Chappell
Little Mary Sunshine	French	Musical Celebration, A	Chappell
Little Me	Musicscope	My Fair Lady	Musicscope
Little Michus	Litter	My Lady Frayle	French
Little Nellie Kelly	Littler	My Lady Molly	NODA
Little Night Music, A	Weinberger		
Little Princess	French	Naughty Marietta	Richmond
Lock up your Daughters	French	Nautch Girl, The	Dance
Lost in the Stars	Chappell	New Moon, The	Chappell

Title	Copyright owners (or controllers of performing rights)	Title	Copyright owners (or controllers of performing rights)
Night in Venice, A	Weinberger	Pip	NODA
Nina Rosa	French	Pipe Dream	Chappell
No, No, Nanette	French	Pippin	Weinberger
No Strings	Chappell	Pirates of Penzance, The	No performing fee
Not in Front of the Waiter	Chappell	Policeman's Serenade, The	Elkin
		Pompadour	Littler
		Poupée, La	French
O Marry Me	Chappell	Please Teacher	French
Oh, Kay!	Musicscope	Primrose	Littler
Oh! Oh! Delphine	French	Princess Charming	French
Oh! Susannah	Richmond	Princess Cyrice	French
Oklahoma!	Chappell	Princess Ida	No performing fee
Old Chelsea	French	Princess of Kensington, A	Chappell
Oliver!	Musicscope	Privates on Parade	French
On the Twentieth Century	French	Promises, Promises	Musicscope
Once upon a Mattress	Weinberger		
One Night in Venice	Richmond	Quaker Girl, The	Littler
Orpheus in the Underworld	Weinberger	Rainbow Inn	French
Our Man in Havana	Weinberger	Rebel Maid, The	Chappell
Our Miss Gibbs	Littler	Red Mill, The	Musicscope
Over She Goes	NODA	Return to the Land of Oz	Richmond
		Rio Rita	French
Pacific Overtures	Weinberger	Riverwind	Weinberger
Paganini	Glocken Verlag	Roar of the Greasepaint . . .	Musicscope
Pajama Game, The	Chappell	Robber Bridegroom, The	Weinberger
Paint Your Wagon	Chappell	Rock Nativity, A	Weinberger
Pal Joey	Chappell	Rocky Horror Show, The	French
Passion Flower	Keith Prowse	Rodgers and Hart	
Patience	No performing fee	(a musical celebration)	Chappell
Paul Jones	Aschelberg	Romany Maid, The	NODA
Pearl Girl	French	Rose-Marie	French
Penelope Anne	French	Rose of Araby	NODA
Perchance to Dream	French	Rose of Persia	D'Oyly Carte
Perichole, La	Weinberger	Rose of the Border	NODA
Peter Pan	French	Ruddigore	No performing fee
Philemon	Weinberger	Runaway Girl, The	Littler
Pickwick	French	Runaways	French
Pink Champagne	French		
Pinnochio	Weinberger	Salad Days	French

Title	Copyright owners (or controllers of performing rights)	Title	Copyright owners (or controllers of performing rights)
Sally	Littler	Sunny	Chappell
San Toy	Littler	Sweeney Todd, the Demon	
Savoyards, The	Boosey & Hawkes	Barber of Fleet Street	Weinberger
Scrooge	Weinberger	Sweet Charity	Musicscope
Secret Life of Walter		Sweet Yesterday	French
Mitty, The	French	Sweethearts	Weinberger
Seven	French	Sybil	Littler
1776	Weinberger		
Shop Girl, The	Littler	Tales of Hoffman, The	Cramer
Shot in the Dark, A	Chappell	Tantivy Towers	Cramer
Show Boat	Chappell	Tarantara! Tarantara!	French
Silver Patrol	French	Teahouse of the August	
Silver Wings	French	Moon	Chappell
Snow Queen	Weinberger	Tell Me More	Littler
So This is Love	NODA	1066 and all that	French
Soldier	Chappell	The Me that Nobody	
Song of Norway	Chappell	Knows	French
Song of the Sea	French	Them Thar Hills	Allen
Song of the South	NODA	There and Back	NODA
Songbook	French	Thespis	Belwin Mills
Sorcerer, The	No performing fee	They're Playing our Song	French
Sound of Music, The	Chappell	Three Little Maids	Littler
South Pacific	Chappell	Three Musketeers, The	Chappell
Southern Maid, A	Littler	Thumberlina	Chappell
Sporting Love	NODA	Tin Pan Ali!	Weinberger
Springtime	NODA	Tina	Littler
Starting Here, Starting		Tom Jones	Chappell
Now	Weinberger	Tom Sawyer	Weinberger
Stingiest Man in		Tonight's the Night	Littler
Town, The	Weinberger	Toreador, The	Littler
Stop the World, I want		Treasure Island	Weinberger
to get off	Musicscope	Trelawney	French
Street Scene	Chappell	Trial by Jury	No performing fee
Street Singer, The	French	Tulip Time	French
Strider	French	Two Bouquets, The	French
Student Love	French	Two by Two	Chappell
Student Prince, The	Musicscope	Two Gentlemen of Verona	Musicscope
Suburban Strains	French		
Sugar Candy	NODA	Utopia Limited	No performing fee
Summer Song	French		

Title	Copyright owners (or controllers of performing rights)	Title	Copyright owners (or controllers of performing rights)
Vagabond King, The	French		
Valley of Song	Weinberger		MUSICALS FOR YOUNG PEOPLE
Véronique	Littler	Aesop's Fables	Stacey
Vie Parisienne, La	Weinberger	Alan and the King's	
Viktoria and her Hussar	French	Daughters	French
Virginia	French	Alice in Wonderland	Stacey
Viva Mexico	Weinberger	Androcles and the Lion	Stacey
		Beowulf	French
Walking Happy	French	Brer Rabbit	Richmond
Waltz Dream, A	Weinberger	Brother's Ruin	Clevedon
Waltz of my Heart	French		
Waltz Time	French	Carrots	EMI
Waltz Without End	French	Christmas all over the	
Waltzes from Vienna	Weinberger	Place	Stacey
Water Gipsies, The	French	Christmas Carol, A	French
Wedding in Paris, A	French		
West Side Story	Weinberger	Dancing Donkey, The	Stacey
Where's Charley?	French	Dickens Christmas Carol	
Whirled into Happiness	Littler	Show	Stacey
White Horse Inn	French	Dracula Spectacular, The	French
Whittington	Cramer	Dragon for Dinner	French
Who's Hooper?	Littler		
Wild Grows the Heather	French	Flibberty and the Penguin	French
Wild Violets	Chappell	Frog Prince, The	Richmond
Wiz, The	French		
Wizard of Oz, The	Weinberger	Geni of the Golden Key,	
Wonderful Town	Musicscope	The	French
Working	Weinberger	Gingerbread Man	French
Worzel Gummidge	French	Golden Fleece	Stacey
		Good Grief, a Griffin	Stacey
Yeomen of the Guard,		Good Witch of Boston	Stacey
The	No performing fee		
Yes, Madam	French	Hansel and Gretal	Richmond
Your Own Thing	Musicscope	Hijack over Hygenia	French
		I Sincerely Doubt that	
Zip Goes a Million	Littler	this Old House is	
Zoo, The	Cramer	Very Haunted	Stacey
		Jenny and the Lucky Bags	French
		Just So Stories	Stacey
		Larry the Lamb in	
		Toyland	French

Title	Copyright owners (or controllers of performing rights)
Lost and Found Christmas	Stacey
Near-sighted Knight and the Far-sighted Dragon	Stacey
Nutcracker Sweet	French
Otter Bay	Piper
Owl and the Pussycat went to see . . .	French
Papertown Chase, The	French
Pegora the Witch	Stacey
People and Robbers of Cardemon Town	Stacey
Plain Princess	Stacey
Plotters of Cabbage Patch Corner	French
Prince and the Pauper, The	French
Punch and Judy	Stacey
Rags to Riches	Stacey
Riddle me Ree	Stacey
Rockafella	French
Rumpelstiltskin	Richmond
Runaway	Stacey
Runaway Presents	Stacey
Sacramento Fifty Miles	Stacey
Star-Spangled Minstrel	Stacey
Steal Away Home	Stacey
Sweeney Todd Shock 'n' Roll Show, The	French
There was an Old Woman	French

Title	Copyright owners (or controllers of performing rights)
Tom Sawyer	Stacey
Trudi and the Minstrel	Stacey
Ulysses	French
Wiggle Worms Surprise	Stacey
Wonderful Tang	Stacey
Yankee Doodle	Stacey

PANTOMIME WRITERS AND THEIR AGENTS

Leonard H. Caddy	NODA
Geoffrey Clarke	NODA
John Crocker	French
Ron Hall	NODA
Jack F. Hilton	NODA
Michael Hollingsworth	NODA
Mary Howarth	NODA
Emile Littler (various)	Littler
Edmund Lyon	NODA
Wilfred Miller	NODA
John Moreley	French
Verne Morgan	NODA/French
Ronald Parr	French
Peter Quartermaine & Clarkson Rose	Richmond
Robert Rutherford	NODA
K.O. Samuel	French
Johnny Scott	Pantomime King
Barry Stacey	Richmond
David Wood	French

Addresses of Publishers, Rights' Holders or Agents

Belwin Mills Music Ltd, Dept. M, 250 Purley Way, Surrey CR9 4QD
Boosey & Hawkes Ltd, 295 Regent Street, London WIR 8JH (01–580 2060)
Chappell Music Ltd, 129 Park Street, London WIY 3FA (01–629 7600)
Clevedon Printing Co Ltd, Six Ways, Clevedon, Avon, BS21 7SW
J.B. Cramer & Co Ltd, 99 St Martin's Lane, London WC2N 4AZ (01–240 1612)

EMI Education Dept., 21 Denmark Street, London WC2H 8NE (01–836 6699)

Samuel French Ltd, 52–6 Fitzroy Street, London W1P 5HS (01–387 9373)

Ron Hall, 47 Pasture Lane, Seamer, Scarborough

Keith Prowse Music Publishing Co Ltd, 138 Charing Cross Road, London WC2 (01–836 6699)

Emile Littler Musical Plays, Palace Theatre, Shaftesbury Avenue, London WIV 8AY (01–437 3890)

Donald Madgwick, 11 Quadrant Road, Thornton Heath, Surrey CR4 7DB (01–684 1812)

Musicscope Ltd, 42 Cranbourn Street, London WC2H 7AN (01–434 1000)

NODA, 1 Crestfield Street, London WC1H 8AU (01–837 5655)

Novello & Co Ltd, 27 Soho Square, London W1 (01–437 1222)

Pantomime King, 103 Hawthorn Drive, Ipswich, Suffolk

Piper Publications, Ash House, Yarnfield, Stone, Staffs. ST15 ONJ (0785 760518)

Richmond Music Co, 95 Vardon Drive, Leigh-on-Sea, Essex

Stacey Publications, 1 Hawthorndene Road, Hayes, Bromley, Kent BR2 7DZ (01–462 6461)

Josef Weinberger/Glocken Verlag Ltd, 12–14 Mortimer Street, London WIN 8EL (01–580 2827)

Orchestral parts for Gilbert & Sullivan Operas and other Savoy Operas: The Librarian, D'Oyly Carte Library, 20 Stukely Street, London WC1 (01–405 2030)

Part B

Whilst every care has been taken to ensure the accuracy of these entries, the reader is advised to check by telephone before ordering.

COSTUMES

Morris Angel & Son Ltd, 119 Shaftesbury Avenue, London WC2 (01–836 5678)

Art & Archery, 13 Tower Centre, Hoddesdon, Herts – chain armour & leather costumes (01–616 4710)

B & J Costumes, St Helier Avenue, Morden, Surrey – children's costumes (01–648 2790)

Bermans & Nathans Ltd, 18 Irving Street, London WC2 (01–839 1651) (Stores) 40 Camden Street, London NW1 (01–387 0999)

Birmingham Repertory Theatre Hire Dept., Oozells Street, Birmingham B1 2EP (01–643 6034)

Black Lion Costumes, 1 Fairlawn Road, Montpelier, Bristol BS6 5JR (0272–41345)

Brandons (Theatrical Costumiers), Dower House Flat, Coopers Lane, Northaw, Potters Bar, Herts (77–59553)

Brighton Theatrical Costumiers, 34 Upper North Street, Brighton, Sussex (0272–25342)

Bristol Old Vic Hire Service, Colston Hall, Colston Street, Bristol BS1 5AR (0272–291117)

Costume Studio, 227 Eversholt Street, London NW1 (01–388 4481)

Danswear Centre, 5 Dixon Street, Glasgow G1 4AL – dance costumes (041–221 5518)

Dauphine Stage & Hire, 8 West Street, Old Market, Bristol BS2 0HB (0272–551700)

English Armour Hire, 115 George Street, Romford. Essex (01–702 4696)

Fancy Dress Shop, 9 Church Street, Gainsborough, Lincs (0427–616230)

Frederick Freed Ltd, 94 St Martin's Lane, London WC2 – shoes (01–240 0432)

Alan Graham Costumes, 5 Park Road, Consett, Co. Durham (027–509202)

Harveys of Hove, 110–12 Trafalgar Road, Portslade, Sussex BN4 1GS (0272–777467)

Haslemere Wardrobe, St. Christopher's Road, Haslemere, Surrey (0428–2202)

J. Hill Theatrical Costume Hire, 50 Highfields Road, Hinckley, Leics. LE10 1UU (0455–616059)

Hilworth Costumes, 46 Lees Lane, Southoe, Huntingdon, Cambs

W.A. Homburg Ltd, King House, Sovereign Street, Leeds LS1 4BU (0532–458425)

Karnival Costumes, 732–4 Woodborough Road, Mapperley, Nottingham (0602–602887)

Joker Costumes Hire, 97 Chiswick High Road, London W4 2ED (01–995 4118)

Judy Lambert Theatrical Costume Hire, 7 Station Road, Belmont, Surrey (01–661 9198)

Lawrence Corner, 62–4 Hampstead Road, London NW1 – Government surplus & military

Lawrence Corner Him & Hers Boutique, 126–30 Drummond Street, London NW1

Lyndon Theatrical Costume Hire, 16–18 Hamlet Court Road, Westcliff-on-Sea, Essex (0702–42964)

Marigold Costumes, Brynmawr, Gwent (0495–310138)

Northern Theatre Co (Margaret Taylor), 32 Woodland Drive, Anlaby, Hull, N. Humberside (0482–656281)

Northprops (Costume Hire), The Old Police Station, Station Road, Sowerby Bridge, West Yorkshire (0422–33577)

Betty & Sheila Robbins, The Old Fire Station, 40 George Street, Oxford OX1 2AQ (0865–40268)

Nellie Smith, 190 Mansfield Road, Nottingham (0602–64452)

Star Costumes, 78 Elms Road, London SW4 9EW (01–622 6401/2)

Terrington & Lamb, 41 Beckett Road, Doncaster DN2 4AD (0302–28420)

Theatre Zoo Ltd, 28 New Row, St Martin's Lane, London WC2N 4LA (01–836 3150) 21 Earlham Street, London WC2H 9LL – animal costumes

Theatrical Costume House (Westcliff) Ltd, 85–9 Queen's Road, Southend-on-Sea, Essex (0702–332722)

Utopia Costumes, Utopia House, High Street, Broughton, Stockbridge, Hants (079–430 573)

Watkins & Cie Stage Shop, 177–9 Newcastle Street, Stoke on Trent, Staffs (0782–811886)

S.B. Watts & Co Ltd, Princess House, 144 Princess Street, Manchester M1 7EN (061–273 2683)

Robert White & Sons, 22 Tavistock Street, London WC2E 7PY – armour (01–836 8237)

FURNITURE & FURNISHINGS

Crucible Theatre, 55 Norfolk Street, Sheffield S1 1DA (0742–760621)

J.C. Farley, 1–5 Brunel Road, London W3 7UG (01–749 6668)

Gimbert's Ltd, Victoria Mill, Manchester Road, Droylsden, Manchester M35 6EQ (061–370 2232)

Louis Koch & Son, 106 Cleveland Street, London W1 (01–387 8426)

Old Times Furnishing Co., 135 Lower Richmond Road, London SW15 (01–788 3551)

Studio & TV Hire Ltd, Farm Lane, London SW6 1PP (01–381 3511)

LIGHTING EQUIPMENT

AJS Lighting Services, 27 Aylmer Grove, Newton Aycliffe, Co. Durham DL5 4NF (0325–314946)

AJS Theatre Lighting & Stage Supplies Ltd, 15 Kilmarnock Road, Winton, Bournemouth, Dorset BH9 1NP (0202–532031)

Ancient Lights, 8 West Carr Road, Attleborough, Norfolk NR17 1AA (0953–452210)

Berkey Colotran, PO Box 5, Burrell Way, Thetford. Norfolk IP24 3RB (Thetford 2484)

Bourke Strand Electric Ltd, 30 Upper Abbey Street, Dublin 1, Eire

CGT Theatre Lighting Ltd, Windsor House, 26 Willow Lane, Mitcham, Surrey CR4 4NA (01–640 3366)

   1 Wilson Street, Bristol BS2 9HH (0272–462137)

Cleveland (Film & Television) Lighting, Unit 84, Teesside Airport, Darlington, Co. Durham (Dimsdale 2988)

Concord Theatre Lighting Ltd, 607 London Road, North Cheam, Surrey (01–337 8505)

CTL (Control Technology) Ltd, 2 Cornwallis Road, Maidstone, Kent ME16 8BA (0622–65680)

Dominic Light & Sound Ltd, 1–5 Christopher Place, Chalton Street, London NW1 1JF (01–388 2936)

Donmar Sales & Hire, 39 Earlham Street, London WC2H 9LD (01–836 3221)

Philip L. Edwards (Theatre Lighting), 5 Highwood Close, Glossop, Derbyshire SK13 9PH (04574–62811)

W.J. Furse & Co Ltd, Traffic Street, Nottingham NG2 1NF (0602–868213)

Futurist Theatrical Hire Ltd, Blakeridge Mill, Blakeridge Lane, Batley, West Yorks (0924–475590)

Green Ginger Ltd, 52 Potters Lane, Kiln Farm, Milton Keynes MK1 3HQ (0908–566170)

David Hersey Associates Ltd, 162 Anyards Road, Cobham, Surrey KT11 2LH – gobos (Cobham 7117)

Lancelyn Lighting (Oxford), 112 Walton Street, Oxford (0865–511522)

Le Maitre Lighting, 316 Purley Way, Croydon, Surrey – dry ice, smoke cartridges (01–686 9258)

Lee Filters Ltd, Walworth Industrial Estate, Andover, Hants SP10 5AN (0264–66245)

Robert Luff Theatrical Hire Ltd, 36–8 Gautrey Road, Nunhead SE15 2JQ (01–639 6911)

Northern Light, 39–41 Assembly Street, Leith, Edinburgh EH6 7RG (031–553 2383)

Northern Light, 134 St Vincent Street, Glasgow G2 5JU (041–248 5735)

Playlight Hire Ltd, Sovereign Works, Church Lane, Lowton, nr Warrington (0942–73077)

Playlight Hire Ltd, 39a Nottingham Road, Kegworth, nr Derby (05097–3266)

Rank Strand, PO Box 51, Great West Road, Brentford TW8 9HR (01–568 9222)

Rank Strand/MM Stage Electrics, 84 Mina Road, St Werburghs, Bristol

Roscolab Ltd, 69–71 Upper Ground, London SE1 9PQ (01–633 9220)

Stage Audio Visual Enterprises, Hilfield Farm House, Hilfield Lane, Aldenham, Watford, Herts WD2 8DD (01–950 5986)

Stage Control Ltd, Station Parade, Whitchurch Lane, Edgware HA8 6RW (01–952 5986)

Theatre Projects Services Ltd, 10–16 Mercer Street, London WC2 (01–240 5411)

Theatre Sound & Lighting (Services Ltd), Queen's Theatre, 51 Shaftesbury Avenue, London W8V 8BA (01–439 2441)

Theatrelights, 15 High Street, Rampton, Cambridge CB4 4QE (0954–50851)

Thorn Lighting Ltd, Theatre Lighting Division, Angel Road Works, 402 Angel Road, Edmonton N18 3AJ (01–807 9011)

Travelling Light (Birmingham) Ltd, 177 Rookery Road, Handsworth, Birmingham, West Midlands B21 9QZ (021–523 3297)

MAKEUP AND WIGS

'Bert' (Wigs), 28 New Row, St Martin's Lane, London WC2N 4LA (01–836 3150)

Brandons Ltd, The Dower House Annexe, Northaw, Potters Bar, Herts (01–775 9553)

Brighton Theatrical Costumiers, 34 Upper North Street, Brighton, Sussex (0273–25342)

Dance & Theatrical Supplies, 7 Castlefields, Main Centre, Derby DE1 2PE (0332–48062)

Dauphine Stage & Hire, 8 West Street, Old Market, Bristol BS2 0HB (0272–551700)

Fancy Dress Shop, 9 Church Street, Gainsborough, Lincs (0427–616230)

Charles H. Fox Ltd, 22 Tavistock Street, London WC2E 7PY (01–240 3111)

Alan Graham Costumes, 5 Park Road, Consett, Co. Durham (027–509202)

Harlequinade of Chorley, 51 Union Street, Chorley, Lancs (Chorley 77169)

W. A. Homburg Ltd, King House, Sovereign Street, Leeds LS1 4BU (0532–458425)

Warren Landsfield (Wigs), 47 Glenmore Road, London NW3 4DA (01–722 4581)

Lyndon Theatrical Costume Hire, 16–20 Hamlet Court Road, Westcliff-on-Sea, Essex (0702–42964)

Theatre Zoo Ltd, 28 New Row, St Martin's Lane, London WC2N 4LA (01–836 3150)

Theatre Zoo Ltd, 21 Earlham Street, London WC2H 9LL

A.B. Watts & Co Ltd, Princess House, 144 Princess Street, Manchester M1 7EN (061–273 2683)

Wig Creations, 12 Old Burlington Street, London W1X 2PX (01–734 7381)

Wig Specialities Ltd, 173 Seymour Place, London W1H 5TP (01–262 6565)

PROPERTIES

Bapty & Co Ltd, 703 Harrow Road, London NW10 – weapons & firearms (01–696 6671/2)

Barnum's Carnival Novelties, 67 Hammersmith Road, London W14 (01–602 1211)

Birmingham Repertory Theatre Hire Dept, Oozells Street, Birmingham B1 2EP (021–643 6034)

Bristol Old Vic Hire Service, Colston Hall, Colston Street, Bristol BS1 5AR (0272–291117)

George Cook Fan Hire Service, 'Havenhurst', Back Lane, East Hanningfield, Chelmsford CM3 5BL (0245–400519)

Leon Cooper, 10 Station Road, Batley, West Yorkshire (0924–475057)

J.C. Farley, 1–5 Brunel Road, London W3 7UG (01–749 6668)

Gerrard (Hire) Ltd, 85 Royal College Street, London NW1 – stuffed animals, etc (01–387 2765)

Howorth Theatrical Supplies, 9 Wheelwright Close, Marple, Stockport SK6 6QD – firearms (061–449 9766)

Ishaque, 28 Harford House, Tavistock Crescent, London W11 1AY – Indian & Pakistani props (01–727 1781)

JMB Hire Co Ltd, 52a Goldhawk Road, London W12 (01–743 7663)

Chris James & Co, 11 New Wharf Road, London N1 9RT – breakaway bottles & glasses (01–837 3062/3)

Keeley (Film & TV Hire) Ltd, 4a Charlton Mead Lane, Hoddesdon, Herts (61–44584)

Richard Kihl Wine Accessories, 164 Regents Park Road, London NW1 8XN (01–586 3838)

Louis Koch & Son, 106 Cleveland Street, London W1 (01–387 8426)

Low Cost Props, 69 Dundas Street, Edinburgh (031–556 4288)

Mend-a-Bike, 13 Park Walk, London SW10 (01–352 3999) and 917 Fulham Road, London SW6 (01–736 8655) – vintage & modern bike hire

Mooredan Hire Ltd, Unit 2, Central Park Estate, Staines Road, Hounslow TW4 5DT (01–572 2121)

Mostly Metal, 5a Uxbridge Road, London W12 8LJ (01–743 6210)

Old Times Furnishing Co, 135 Lower Richmond Road, London SW15 (01–788 3551)

Props Galore, 62 Blythe Road, London W14 (01–602 1922)

Rent-a-Sword, 180 Frog Grove Lane, Wood Street Village, Guildford, Surrey (048–642 2284)

Stage-Craft Jewellery Hire, 'Brigadoon', Barrack Road, West Parley, Wimbourne, Dorset BH22 8UB (0202–57286)

Studio & TV Hire Ltd, Farm Lane, London SW6 1PP (01–381 3511)

Theatre Zoo Ltd, 28 New Row, St Martin's Lane, London WC2N 4LA (01–836 3150) 21 Earlham Street, London WC2H 9LL

Robert White & Sons, 22 Tavistock Street, London WC2E 7PY – armour, jewellery, swords (01–240 3111)

SCENERY

Clifford & Brown, Weddington Industrial Estate, Weddington Terrace, Nuneaton CV10 0AG (0682–66742)

James Fredericks, Scenic Studios, Langford Road, Weston-super-Mare, Somerset (0934–24791)

Northern Theatre Co. (Margaret Taylor), 32 Woodland Drive, Anlaby, Hull, North Humberside (0482–656281)

Russell & Chapple Ltd, 23 Monmouth Street, London WC2H 9DE

Say Bloxham, Fore Street, Kingskerwell, Newton Abbot, Devon (080–47 2386)

The Stage Productions Co Ltd, The Hall, Camden Park Road, London NW1 9AY (01–485 3309)

Stagesets (London), 22–4 & 42–3a Peto Street South, London E16 1AJ (01–476 1019)

SOUND

Albatross Sound Services Ltd, Strand Theatre, Aldwych, London WC2 (01–240 3142)

Robert Luff Theatrical Hire Ltd, 36–8 Gautrey Road, Nunhead, London SE15 2JQ (01–732 2015)

Mac Sound Hire, 15 Park Street, Swinton, Manchester M27 1UG (061–794 1888)

Northern Light, 39–41 Assembly Street, Leith, Edinburgh EH6 7RG (031–553 2383)

Northern Light, 134 St Vincent Street, Glasgow G2 5JU (041–248 5735)

Optical & Textile Ltd, 22–6 Victoria Road, New Barnet, Herts EN4 9PF (01–441 2199)

Theatre Projects Services Ltd, 10–16 Mercer Street, London WC2 (01–240 5411)

Theatre Sound & Lighting (Services) Ltd, Queen's Theatre, Shaftesbury Avenue, London W1V 8BA (01–439 2441)

MISCELLANEOUS SUPPLIES

Amateur Stage, Block Hire Dept., 1 Hawthorndene Road, Hayes, Bromley, Kent BR2 7DZ – illustrated programme blocks (01–462 6461)

British Theatre Association, 9 Fitzroy Square, London W1P 6AE – library, information, records (01–387 2666)

Brodie & Middleton Ltd, 68 Drury Lane, London WC2B 5SP – scenic supplies (01–836 3289)

City Directa Ltd, Cold Norton, Essex CM3 6VA – stage masking tapes, etc (0621–828882)

Concept Engineering Ltd, 30 White Waltham Airfield Estates, Maidenhead, Berks – smoke, fog, etc (062–882 5555)

DHA Lighting, 162 Anyards Road, Cobham, Surrey – gobos (Cobham 7117)

Lewis Davenport & Co, 51 Great Russell Street, London WC1 – magic, tricks (01–405 8524)

Eugene's Flying Ballet, 71 Boltons Lane, Pyrford, Woking, Surrey (91 41616)

French's Theatre Bookshop, 52–6 Fitzroy Street, London W1P 5HS – British, French, German & American sound effects; catalogue available (01–387 9373)

Grandstand Tribunes Ltd, 40 High Street, Stratford-upon-Avon, Warwickshire CV37 6AU – seat hire (0789 67413)

Guardian Royal Exchange Assurance Group, Princess House, 4–10 Eastlake Walk, Drake Circus, Plymouth PL1 1JR – official insurers to NODA (0752–21181)

Rex Howard Ltd, 321 The Vale, Uxbridge Road, London W3 7QS – curtains & equipment for hire or sale (01–749 2958)

Kirby's Flying Ballets, 10 Berriedale Avenue, Hove, Sussex BN3 4JH (0273–737133)

Musisca Ltd, 27 Fore Street, Torsham, nr Exeter, Devon EX3 6HD – stacking music stands (039287–5855)

National Operatic & Dramatic Association, 1 Crestfield Street, London WC1H 8AU – library, scores (01–837 5655)

P & G Draperies Ltd, 15 Park Street, Swinton, Manchester – drapes & soft furnishings (061–793 5848)

D.I. Purdie Ltd, 18 High Street, Lincoln – pyrotechnics (0522–20746)

Roscolab Ltd, 69 Upper Ground, London SE1 – non-irritant fog & smoke system (01–633 9220)

Venyflex Hire, 1 Holly Road, Hampton Hill, Middlesex – drapes, tabs, blinds for hire (01–977 3780)

Glossary

ACT DROP   A painted cloth or curtain that can be lowered at the end of each act

ACTING AREA   (a) The part of the stage whereon the action of the play takes place; (b) Overhead lanterns illuminating the acting area

ALIVE   Piece of scenery or property in use or still required

APRON   The extension of the stage projecting in front of the proscenium arch. Also referred to as 'apron stage' or 'fore-stage'

ARENA STAGE   An open stage where the audience sits all around it

ASIDE   Lines spoken to the audience, yet not intended to be heard by the other players on the stage

A.S.M.   Assistant stage manager

AT RISE   The stage when ready for the rise of the curtain

AUDITORIUM   The part of the theatre where the audience is seated to watch the performance

BACKCLOTH or BACKDROP. A painted canvas sheet, battened top and bottom, and hung from the grid or roof, and used as a backing to a scene.

BACKING   Scenery used behind openings, doors, windows etc., to limit the audience's view

BACK-PROJECTION   Scenic effects projected on to the rear of a cloth

BACK-STAGE   The area behind the proscenium arch, including the dressing rooms, workshops and the stage itself. *See also* FRONT OF HOUSE

BAR or BARREL   Length of metal pipe suspended on a set of lines used for scenery or lanterns. A standard part of the counterweight system

BATTEN   (a) A length of timber or pipe, suspended from a set of lines to which scenery is attached for flying;   (b) A length of timber used to stiffen a hanging cloth at its lower edge;   (c) Any length of wood used in scenery construction;   (d) Overhead length of metal troughing containing lamps in compartments

BARN DOOR   A device for limiting the spread of a beam of light from lanterns

BASTARD PROMPT   When the stage manager's control desk, and thus the prompt, is situated on the OP side of the stage it is termed a 'Bastard Prompt'

BOAT TRUCK   Low, free-moving trolley on which scenery can be pre-set for quick changes. *See also* DOLLY

BOBBIN   Cylindrical carrier for the suspension and movement of draw curtains on a horizontal track

BOOK-CEILING   A hinged ceiling piece (rarely used in musicals)

BOOK FLAT   A pair of hinged flats

BOOK-WING   Constructed and set as a book-flat. Often used in exteriors

BOOM   An upright barrel upon which lanterns are fixed. Used for cross-lighting

BORDER   A strip of canvas suspended from above and used to mask the upper part of the stage, and the lanterns. Often painted to represent foliage or sky. Each is numbered, starting at the proscenium arch. Many modern shows tend to ignore the question of masking the stage mechanics and leave lighting and flying equipment in full view

BOX SET   A series of flats, joined to give a three-sided interior scene.

BRACE   (a) Piece of wood inserted diagonally into the frame of a flat to strengthen it;   (b) An adjustable device, made of two lengths of wood, which can be attached to a flat by a hook at the top, and fixed to the floor with a stage screw or weight, for the purpose of keeping the scenery rigid. Also called a 'stage brace'. *See also* FRENCH BRACE

BRACE-WEIGHT   Slotted iron weight, which can be set on the foot-iron of a brace to hold it in position. Used instead of a stage screw

BRAIL   To move a cloth or other suspended scenery forwards, backwards or laterally, by attaching a horizontal line to the vertical lines from which it is suspended

BUSINESS   Stage action as opposed to dialogue

CARPET CUT   A narrow trap at the front of the stage, used to secure the front edge of a carpet or floor cloth

CENTRE LINE   The line bisecting the stage from front to back. Shown on the ground plans

CLEAT   A wooden or metal attachment on the back of a flat for securing the throwline. Also found affixed to the fly rail for tying off the hemp lines

CLOTH   Any hanging canvas scenery. *See also* CUTCLOTH, STAGE CLOTH

COUNTERWEIGHT SYSTEM   A mechanical method of balancing the weight of scenery to be hung from the grid, for ease of operation

CRADLE   Housing for counterweights

CURTAIN LINE   An imaginary line which marks the position of the house tabs when closed, or lowered.

CUTCLOTH   A cloth which has a part cut away to show another set behind. Often painted to represent trees or foliage. Sometimes the cut-away portion is filled with gauze

CYCLORAMA   A plain curved backing to the stage; either a permanent structure or a stretched cloth used to represent the sky and giving an illusion of infinity.

DEAD   (a) A term used when a border or a piece of suspended scenery is at its correct position in the setting;   (b) A term used when a piece of scenery or property is no longer required. The converse is ALIVE

DIMMER   General term for the appliances by which the quantity of light can be adjusted

DIPS   Small traps in the stage floor containing plug sockets for electrical units

DOCK   The scene store at the side or rear of the stage with direct access to the street for unloading

DOLLY *See* TRUCK

DOOR FLAT A flat into which a door unit can be fitted

DOOR UNIT Practical door in a wooden frame that can be filled into a flat

DOWNSTAGE Nearest the audience

DRAPES Any fabric hanging in folds as a scene, or part of a scene. Also casement and window curtains

DRAW TABS Curtains which open by being drawn to the sides

DROP CURTAIN *See* ACT DROP

FALSE PROSCENIUM Temporary proscenium set within the proscenium opening to lessen the height and width of the stage. In America called the 'show portal'

FESTOON TABS A curtain with several lines passing through rings sewn to webbing on the upstage side, which when raised hangs in swags

FIRE CURTAIN *See* SAFETY CURTAIN

FLAT Unit of scenery – wooden frame covered with canvas

FLIES Fly floor or flying gallery. The narrow gallery above the stage, often on both side walls, from whence the ropes used to fly the scenery are operated. Sometimes a fly bridge across the back wall connects the fly floors

FLIPPER A small piece of flat scenery, hinged to a larger flat

FLOATS The footlights

FLY RAIL Railing on the stage side of the fly floor to which the lines are made off on a cleat

F.O.H. (a) Front of House – the vestibules and foyer of the theatre; (b) Spotlights in the auditorium used to illuminate the stage

FORESTAGE *See* APRON

FRENCH BRACE Wooden support hinged to a flat

FRENCH FLAT Two or three flats battened together for flying

GAUZE Fine woven mesh which can be painted or dyed to look solid when lit from the front. When lit only from behind it appears transparent

GRID Steel framework above the stage from which scenery and lighting is suspended

GROUND PLAN Scale plan of the stage showing the position of scenery in a setting

GROUND ROW Low piece of flat scenery, often with profiled edge, painted to represent middle or far distance. Useful to conceal lighting units for a backcloth, cyclorama etc.

HOUSE TABS The main curtains between the stage and the auditorium

INSET A small scene within a larger one

IRON *See* SAFETY CURTAIN

JOG Narrow flat used as a return to give the illusion of solidarity

LEG A length of canvas or material used as a wing. Curtain sets are made up of tabs, legs and borders

LINES (Set of) The unit group of suspension lines hanging from the grid and used for flying the scenery and lighting. Usually three to a set, and known as the short, centre and long line, reading from the fly rail

MASK To close the gaps in a setting by adjusting backings, borders, wings, legs etc., from the viewpoint of the most extreme sightlines

OFFSTAGE   Any portion of the stage outside the audience's field of vision

ON STAGE   Any part of the stage within the acting area

O.P.   Opposite prompt. Stage right from the actor's viewpoint

PACK   A stack of scenery in the wings ready for use

PERCH   Downstage spotlight behind the side of the proscenium, usually above head height

PIN HINGE   A hinge with a removeable pin so that the two halves can be easily separated

PRACTICAL   Capable of being used for its apparent function, e.g. an actual window as opposed to a painted one

PRIMING   Preparatory coat of size and paint on new canvas, or obliterating coat on an old canvas to be repainted

PROFILE FLAT   Flat with plywood edge cut in silhouette

P.S.   Prompt side. Stage left

PROPERTIES   Props. All objects used on stage that cannot be regarded as costumes or scenery

PROSCENIUM   Pros. The proscenium opening and its surrounding treatment. Theoretically the 'fourth wall' of the stage

RAKE   Slope, either of the whole stage or of a ramped rostrum

RETURN   A flat that leads the downstage edge of a setting 'off' stage

REVEAL   A piece of timber or other material fixed to the edge of an opening to give the impression of thickness

ROSTRUM   A platform

SAFETY CURTAIN   A fire-resistant shutter or curtain mounted immediately behind the proscenium. Usually made of a steel framework faced with iron or asbestos. It has a quick release device to enable it to be lowered speedily in the event of a fire

SET PIECE   A built-up unit of free-standing scenery, often three-dimensional

SETTING LINE   An imaginary line, parallel to the footlights and upstage of the house curtain from which the setting of scenery is measured. Must be shown on the designer's plan

SILL   Flat metal strip used to brace the bottom of a door or arch

SPOT BAR   Barrel, usually counterweighted, from which spotlights are hung over the stage

SPOTLINE   A single line, dropped from the grid. Often used for chandeliers

STAGE CLOTH   Large piece of canvas used to cover the stage floor, often painted to represent marble, paving, grass etc

STAGE SCREW   Large screw for securing stage brace to floor

STILE   The upright member of a flat frame

STRIKE   Take apart and remove a set

TABS   Tableaux curtains. Usually applied to the house curtain but can be hung anywhere

THROWLINE   A line attached to a flat and used to secure it to an adjacent flat

TORMENTOR   Masking flat immediately behind the proscenium, running upstage as far as the setting line or false proscenium

TRAILERS Travelers, traverse or draw curtains

TRANSPARENCY Not a gauze but a cloth or part of a cloth made of linen, which, when painted in dye colours, can be lit from behind

TRAP Trapdoor cut anywhere in the stage floor. Various types include star and grave traps

TRIM To level off a piece of suspended scenery at the right height. Once trimmed it can be 'deaded'

TRIP To raise a cloth using extra lines at the bottom edge so that it can occupy approximately half its height. Used when there is insufficient stage height to fly away normally

TRUCK Wheeled rostrum, carrying setting or part of a setting

WINGS Sides of the stage not in view of the audience

WING SET A set comprising backcloth, wings and borders. Usually an exterior scene and extensively used in the older musicals

Bibliography

Acting and Production Techniques

Albright, Halstead & Mitchell, *Principals of Theatre Art*, Houghton Miflin, 1955.

Albright, Hardie & Arnita, *Acting: The Creative Process*, 3rd edn, Wadsworth, 1980.

Allensworth, Carl, *The Complete Play Production Handbook*, Robert Hale, 1976.

Barkworth, Peter, *About Acting*, Secker & Warburg, 1980.

Boleslavsky, Richard, *Acting: The First Six Lessons*, Theatre Arts, 1949.

Bradbury, Arthur J. et al., *Production & Staging of Plays*, Arco, 1963.

Canfield, Curtis, *The Craft of Play Directing*, Holt Rinehart & Winston, 1963.

Cohen, Robert & Harrop, John, *Creative Play Direction*, Prentice-Hall Inc, 1974.

Colson, Greta, *Drama Skills*, Barrie & Jenkins, 1980.

Curry, Jennifer, *Amateur Theatre* (Teach Yourself Books), Hodder & Stoughton, 1980.

Dean, Alexander & Carra, Lawrence, *The Fundamentals of Play Direction*, 4th edn, Holt Rinehart & Winston, 1980.

Dolman, John jnr, *The Art of Acting*, Harper & Row, 1949.
   The Art of Play Production 3rd edn, Greenwood, 1973.

Fishman, Morris, *The Actor in Training*, Greenwood, 1974.

Gassner, John & Barber, Philip, *Producing the Play with the New Stage Technician's Handbook*, rev. edn, Holt Rinehart & Winston, 1953.

Glenn, Stanley S., *A Director Prepares*, Dickenson, 1973.

Green, Michael, *The Art of Coarse Acting*, rev. edn, Drama Books, 1981.

Griffiths, Trevor R., *Stagecraft: The Complete Guide to Theatrical Practice*, Phaidon, 1983.

Hartmann, Rudolf, *Richard Strauss: The Staging of his Operas & Ballets*, Phaidon, 1980.

Heffner, Hubert C. et al, *Modern Theatre Practice*, 5th edn, Prentice-Hall, 1971.

Hepworth, Martyn, *Amateur Drama: Production & Management*, Batsford, 1978.

Hodge, Francis, *Play Directing: Analysis, Communications & Style*, Prentice-Hall, 1971.

Joseph, Stephen, *Theatre in the Round*, Taplinger, 1968.

King, Nancy, *Theatre Movement: The Actor and his Space*, Drama Books, 1971.

Mackinlay, Leila, *Musical Production*, Herbert Jenkins, 1955.

Matthew, Brian, *Stage Right: How to run an Amateur Theatre Group*, A. & C. Black, 1975.

Miles-Brown, John, *Directing Drama*, Peter Owen, 1980.

Morrison, Hugh, *Directing in the Theatre*, Pitman, 1979.

Oxenford, Lyn, *Playing Period Plays*, Coach House, 1974.
   Design for Movement, Theatre Arts, 1951.

Pisk, Litz, *The Actor and his Body*, Harrap, 1978.

Purdom, C.B., *Producing Plays*, Dent, 1951.

Ramsden, Timothy & Courtice, Pauline, *Stagecraft*, Harrap, 1982.

Reid, Francis, *The Staging Handbook*, Pitman, 1978.

Selbourne, David, *The Making of A Midsummer Night's Dream*, Methuen, 1982.

Seyler, Athene & Haggard, Stephen, *The Craft of Comedy*, Theatre Arts, 1957.

Slade, Peter, *Introduction to Child Drama*, Verry, 1958.

Smethurst, Harold, *Opera Production for Amateurs*, Turnstile, 1951.

Stanislavski, Constantin, *Creating a Role*, Theatre Arts, 1961.

    An Actor Prepares, Theatre Arts, 1948.

    Building a Character, Theatre Arts, 1951.

    Actor's Handbook, Theatre Arts, 1963.

Turfery & Palmer, *The Musical Production*, Pitman, 1953.

Welker, David, *Theatrical Direction*, Allyn, 1971.

Music, Singing, Conducting & the Voice

Aiken, W.A., *The Voice*, Longman, 1963.

Balk, H. Wesley, *The Complete Singer-Actor: Training for the Music Theater*, University of Minnesota Press, 1978.

Berry, Cicely, *Voice and the Actor*, Harrap, 1977

Bowles, Michael, *The Art of Conducting*, Da Capo, 1975.

Cox-Ife, William, *The Elements of Conducting*, John Barker, 1964.

Devito, Joseph A. et al, *Articulation and Voice: Effective Communication*, Bobbs, 1975.

Herbert-Caesari, E., *Vocal Truth*, Robert Hale, 1982.

Kline, Peter, *Theatre Student: The Actor's Voice*, Rosen Press, 1972.

Machlin, Evangeline, *Speech for the Stage*, Theatre Arts, 1980.

    Speech for the Stage: Manual for Class Instruction, Theatre Arts, 1980.

Punt, Norman A., *The Singer & Actor's Throat*, 3rd edn, Drama Books, 1979.

Rose, Arnold, *The Singer & The Voice: Vocal Physiology & Technique for Singers,* 2nd edn, Scolar Press, 1978.

Dancing and Movement

Gelb, Michael, *Body Learning: An Introduction to the Alexander Technique*, Delilah Comm, 1981.

Lawson, Joan, *The Principles of Classical Dance*, A. & C. Black, 1979.

    Beginning Ballet, A. & C. Black, 1980.

    Teaching Young Dancers, A. & C. Black, 1978.

Stage Management

Bellman, W.F., *Scenography & Stage Technology: An Introduction*, Harper & Row, 1977.

Cavanaugh, Jim, *Theatre Student: Organisation & Management of Non-Professional Theatre*, Rosen Press, 1973.

Conberg, Sol & Gebauer, Emanuel L., *A Stage-crew Handbook*, rev. edn, Harper & Row, 1957.
Goffin, Peter, *Art & Science of Stage Management*, Philos, 1953.
Greenberg, Jan W., *Theatre Business: From Auditions Through Opening Night*, Holt Rinehart & Winston, 1981.
McInnes, James, *Video in Education and Training*, Focal Press, 1981.
Robinson, J.F.G. & Beards, P.H., *Using Videotape*, Focal Press, 1976.
Stern, Lawrence, *Stage Management: A Guidebook of Practical Techniques*, 2nd edn, Allyn & Bacon, 1982.

Properties

Bruder, Karl, *Theatre Student: Properties & Dressing the Stage*, Rosen Press, 1969.
Kenton, Warren, *Stage Properties & How to Make Them*, Drama Books, 1978.
Motley, *Theatre Props*, Drama Books, 1976.
Terry, Ellen & Anderson, Lynne, *Theatre Student: Makeup & Masks*, Rosen Press, 1971.

Sound & Effects

Borwick, John, *Sound Recording Practice*, OUP, 1980.
Burris-Meyer, Harold et al, *Sound in the Theatre*, Theatre Arts, 1979.
Collinson, David, *Stage Sound*, Studio Vista, 1976.
Walne, Graham, *Sound for Theatres: A Basic Manual*, John Offord, 1981.

Scenery

Adix, Vern, *Theatre Scenecraft*, Anchorage, 1957.
Buerki, F.A., *Stagecraft for Non-Professionals*, 3rd edn, University of Wisconsin Press, 1972.
Burris-Meyer, Harold & Cole, Edward C., *Scenery for the Theatre*, 2nd edn, Little Brown, 1972.
Corey, Irene, *The Mask of Reality*, Anchorage.
Friederich & Fraser, *Scenery Design for the Amateur Stage*, Macmillan, 1964.
Gillette, A.S., *Stage Scenery: Its Construction & Rigging*, 2nd edn, Harper & Row, 1981.
Huggett, Chris, *Stage Crafts*, A. & C. Black, 1980.
Miller, James Hull, *Self-supporting Scenery*, Stacey.
Nelms, Hennig, *Stage Design: A Guide to the Stage*, Dover, 1975.
Parker, Oren W. & Smith, Harvey K., *Scene Design and Stage Lighting*, 4th edn, Holt Rinehart & Winston, 1963.
Polunin, Vladimir, *The Continental Method of Scene Painting*, Dance Books, 1980.
Selden, Samuel & Rezzuto, Tom, *Essentials of Stage Scenery*, Prentice-Hall, 1972.
Southern, Richard, *Stage-setting for Amateurs & Professionals*, Faber & Faber, 1964.
Stell, Joseph W., *Theatre Student: Scenery*, Rosen Press, 1970.

Stoddard, Richard, *Stage Scenery, Machines & Lighting*, Gale Research, 1977.
Warre, Michael, *Designing & Making Stage Scenery*, Studio Vista, 1966.
Welker, David, *Stagecraft*, Allyn & Bacon, 1978.
   Theatre Set Design: The Basic Techniques, 2nd edn, Allyn & Bacon, 1979.
Videotape: How to Make Stage Scenery, Parts I & II (£35.00), Oakroyd Television, 57
   Orchard Road, St Anne's on Sea, Lancs FY8 1NJ.

Lighting

Bellman, Willard F., *Lighting the Stage: Art & Practice*, 2nd edn, Chandler, 1964.
Bentham, Frederick, *The Art of Stage Lighting*, 3rd edn, Pitman, 1980.
Bergman, Gosta M., *Lighting in the Theatre*, Rowman, 1977.
Bongar, Emmet, *Theatre Student: Practical Stage Lighting*, Rosen Press, 1971.
Corry, P., *Lighting the Stage*, Pitman, 1964.
Fuchs, Theodore, *Home-built Lighting*, French, 1939.
Goffin, Peter, *Stage Lighting for Amateurs*, J. Garnet Miller, 1952.
Hinton (ed.) et al, *Essentials of Stage*, Prentice-Hall, 1982.
Parker, Oren W. & Smith, Harvey K., *Scene Design & Stage Lighting*, 4th edn, Holt
   Rinehard & Winston, 1963.
Pilbrow, Richard *Stage Lighting*, rev. edn, Studio Vista, 1980.
Reid, Francis, *The Stage Lighting Handbook*, 2nd edn, A. & C. Black, 1982.

Costume

Arnold, Janet, *A Handbook of Costume*, S.G. Phillips, 1974.
   Patterns of Fashion: Englishwomen's Dresses & their Construction, Vol 1 *c*1660–1860,
   3rd edn, Drama Books, 1977.
   Patterns of Fashion: Englishwomen's Dresses & their Construction, Vol 2 *c*1860–1940,
   3rd edn, Drama Books, 1977.
Barton, Lucy, *Western World Costume: An Outline History*, Prentice-Hall, 1954.
Brooke, Iris, *Footwear: A Short History of European & American Shoes*, Theatre Arts,
   1971.
Carson, Richard, *Fashions in Hair: The First 5000 Years,* 3rd edn, Humanities, 1971.
de Marly, Diana, *Costume on Stage 1600–1940*, Batsford, 1982.
Emery, Joy Spanabel, *Stage Costume Techniques*, Prentice-Hall, 1981.
Fernold, Mary & Shenton, Eileen, *Costume Design & Making*, 2nd edn, A. & C. Black,
   1977.
Green, Ruth M., *Costume & Fashion in Colour 1550–1760*, Plays, 1976.
Harrold, Robert & Legg, Phyllida, *Folk Costumes of the World,* Blandford, 1981.
Hope, Thomas, *Costumes of the Greeks & Romans*, rev. edn, Dover.
Ingham, Rosemary & Covey, Elizabeth, *The Costumer's Handbook*, Prentice-Hall,
   1980.
Jackson, Shiela, *Costumes for the Stage*, Herbert Press, 1978.
Kesler, Jackson, *Theatrical Costume: A Guide to Information Sources*, Gale, 1979.

Kybalova et al (trans.), *Pictorial Encyclopaedia of Fashion*, Hamlyn, 1968.
Laver, James, *A Concise History of Fashion*, Thames & Hudson, 1979.
Lister, Margot, *Costume: An Illustrated Survey from Ancient Times to the Twentieth Century*, Plays, 1968.
   Costumes of Everyday Life: An Illustrated History of Working Clothes, Plays, 1972.
Motley, *Designing and Making Stage Costumes*, Studio Vista, 1964.
Russell, Douglas A., *Period Style for the Theatre*, Allyn & Bacon, 1980.
Thomas, Beverly Jane, *A Practical Approach to Costume Design & Construction,* vols 1 & 2 (paper), Allyn & Bacon, 1982.
Yarwood, Doreen, *English Costume*, 4th edn, David & Charles, 1975.
   Costumes of the Western World, St Martin's Press, 1981.
   Encyclopaedia of World Costume, Scribner, 1978.
   European Costume, David & Charles, 1975.

Makeup

Blore, Richard (of Leichner), *Stage Makeup*, Stacey, 1965.
Corson, Richard, *Stage Makeup*, 6th edn, Prentice-Hall, 1981.
Kehoe, Vincent J.R., *The Technique of Film & Television Makeup*, rev. edn, Hastings.
Liszt, Rudolph G., *The Last Word in Makeup*, rev. edn, Dramatist's Play Service, 1980.
Perrottet, Phillippe, *Practical Stage Makeup*, Studio Vista, 1967.
Stanley, Adrian, *A Guide to Greasepaint*, French, 1953.

General Reference

Bailey, Leslie, *The Gilbert & Sullivan Book*, 4th edn, Scholarly.
Barkworth, Peter, *Broadway Musicals*, Abrams, 1980.
Bordman, Gerald, *American Operetta*, OUP, 1981.
Bradley, Ian, *The Annotated Gilbert & Sullivan*, Penguin Books, 1982.
Burris-Meyer, Harold & Cole, Edward C., *Theatre & Auditoriums*, 2nd edn, Krieger, 1975.
Cotterell, Leslie E., *Performance*, John Offord, 1978.
Craig, Edward Gordon, *On the Art of the Theatre*, Theatre Arts, 1956.
Crampton, Esme, *A Handbook of the Theatre*, Heinemann, 1977.
Druxman, Michael, *The Musical from Broadway to Hollywood*, A.S. Barnes, 1980.
Ewen, David, *The Book of European Light Opera*, Greenwood, 1977.
   The Story of America's Musical Theatre, Chilton, 1961.
Green, Stanley, *Encyclopaedia of the Musical*, Cassell, 1977.
Griffiths, Stuart, *How Plays are Made*, Heinemann Educational, 1982.
Hartnoll, Phyllis (ed.), *Oxford Companion to the Theatre*, 3rd edn, OUP, 1967.
Herbert, Ian (ed.), *Who's Who in the Theatre*, 2 vols, 17th edn, Gale.
Hobbs, William, *Stage Combat*, Barrie & Jenkins, 1980.
Jackson, Arthur, *The Book of Musicals*, Mitchell Beazley, 1979.

Katz, *Theatre Student: Stage Violence*, Rosen Press, 1975.

Kernodle, George & Portia, *Invitation to the Theatre*, 2nd edn, Harcourt Brace.

Mackinlay, Sterling, *Origins & Development of Light Opera*, Gordon Press.

McSpaadden, J. Walker, *Opera Synopses*, Folcroft, 1978.

Sennett, Ted, *Hollywood Musicals*, Abrams, 1981.

Stern, Lawrence, *School & Community Theatre Management: A Handbook for Survival*, Allyn & Bacon, 1979.

Swortzell, Cowell & Nancy, *Theatre in Education*, Longman, 1982.

Trevor, Pat, *Professionally Yours*, Brown, Son & Ferguson, 1981.

Williamson, Audrey, *Gilbert & Sullivan Opera*, rev. edn by Marion Boyars, Bowker, 1982.

Useful Periodicals

Amateur Stage, Stacey Publications, Annual Subs £8.50.

British Alternative Theatre Directory, John Offord (Publications), Annually (March) £5.00.

British Theatrical Directory, John Offord (Publications)

Creative Drama, Stacey Publications for Educational Drama Association, Annually £1.00.

Cue, Technical Theatre Review, Twynam Publishing Ltd, Annual Subs £10.50

Dancing Times, Dancing Times Ltd, Monthly 60p, Annual Subs £8.50.

Drama, British Theatre Association, Quarterly (Jan.) 85p., Annual Subs £4.50.

Gilbert & Sullivan Journal, R.C. Giffin, 54 Camborne Road, Morden, Surrey.

Kemp's International Film & TV Directory.

London Drama, Stacey Publications, Spring & Autumn 50p each, Subs £1.50.

London Theatre, Jaguar Press, Monthly £1.00, Subs £10.00.

Musical Opinion, Musical Opinion Ltd, Monthly 70p, Subs £10.40.

Musical Play Parade, free on request to Samuel French Ltd.

NODA News, NODA Ltd, Spring, Summer, Winter.

Opera, Seymour Press, Monthly 75p, Festival Issue £1.00.

Speech & Drama, Society of Teachers of Speech & Drama, Feb, June, Oct. 90p, Subs £2.50.

Spotlight Contacts, The Spotlight, Annual (May).

Tabs, Rank Strand Electric, free on request.

Theatre Crafts, Rodale Press, Pennsylvania 18049, USA, 6 Issues per year.

Theatre Directory, Stacey Publications, £1.50.

Theatre Notebook, Society for Theatre Research, June, May, Sept, Subs £12.00.

Theatrical Research International, OUP, Jan, May, Oct, £6.00, Subs £15.00.

Toneel Teatraal, International Theatre Institute, Herengracht, Amsterdam, 10 issues yearly: 35Hfl per $\frac{1}{2}$ yr.

Index